SOCIETY AND EDUCATION IN ENGLAND SINCE 1800

P. W. Musgrave

METHUEN AND CO LTD 11 New Fetter Lane London EC4

First published in 1968 *by Methuen and Co Ltd*
Reprinted 1969
© 1968 *by P. W. Musgrave*
Printed in Great Britain by
Butler and Tanner Ltd
Frome and London
Paperback   SBN 416 10790 7
Hardback   SBN 416 10780 X
1.2

Distributed in the U.S.A.
by Barnes and Noble Inc.

MODERN TEACHING
Edited by P. W. Musgrave

SOCIETY AND EDUCATION IN ENGLAND SINCE 1800

Contents

Preface

The idea for this book originated in a theoretical paper entitled *A Model for the Analysis of the Development of the English Educational System from 1860* given to the Sociology of Education Section of the Sixth World Congress of Sociology at Evian in 1966.[1] In expanding this paper into a more readable and fuller account I have been helped by the advice of three colleagues at the University of Aberdeen. Firstly, J. C. Kincaid of the Department of Sociology read the first sketch for this book and pointed out the importance of informal agencies of education for a full analysis. Secondly, D. J. Withrington of the Department of History and G. Kirk of the Department of Education read the final version and made a number of detailed suggestions. In addition I am indebted to Malcolm Seaborne of the School of Education, the University of Leicester, for his comments made as a result of an extremely careful reading of the manuscript. Naturally final responsibility rests with me.

Aberdeen   1968   P W M

---

[1] See Transactions, Vol. IV (forthcoming).

Preface to Second Impression

A number of readers have been kind enough to point out several errors in the first printing of this book. I have, therefore, taken the opportunity of a second impression to make a number of minor corrections. I am particularly grateful to Dr Henry Pelling of St John's College, Cambridge, for his help in this matter.

Aberdeen   1969   P W M

CHAPTER ONE

INTRODUCTION

The history of the English educational system has usually been written in one of two ways. Firstly, there are descriptions of how educational institutions have developed over given stretches of time and of the legislation that has governed this growth. Often aspects of the political struggles leading to such legislation are considered. Secondly, there are very detailed investigations of particular institutions or branches of educational endeavour. Sometimes these investigations are related to the social setting in which the institutions existed. But there seems to be a lack of a short, yet broad, examination of the historical development of the English educational system as a social institution that shows the changing inter-relationships of education with such other social institutions as the family, the economy or the social class system. One aim of this brief account is to fill this gap for those students of education, sociology or history who wish to examine the sweep of educational history over the last century and a half. This may be called the academic aim of this book.

There is also a very practical aim. Serving teachers define the situations that they meet in a specific way and act on their definitions. Both the situations and the way that they define them are to a large extent the products of past historical circumstances. Therefore, if teachers are to act efficiently in their positions they must know something of how the system within which they are serving came to be what it is. The history of education

1

has great intrinsic interest to many, especially to those who are professionally concerned with the schools. But the subject has also a practical importance in that a knowledge of it will enable teachers to be more effective in their work, and the practical aim of this book is to enable teachers to be just this by knowing how the English system developed to its present state and what forces are at work on them in the school as they go about their task of teaching children.

The first and more academic aim of examining the development of education as an institution in its social setting can be met by employing a more sociological approach than is usual when considering educational history and basically this book is an essay in historical sociology. The concept of 'the definition of the situation' is central to the method used here. In any institutional sphere, such as education, the definition of what that institution is thought to be at any one time can be discovered from historical sources. Thus Acts of Parliament, the speeches of politicians, administrative regulations and official reports all reveal in some measure how institutions were viewed at the time. In a democratic political system these definitions are usually the end product of a bargaining process. They constitute a truce situation. A study of any particular definition and the circumstances in which it was achieved will reveal the values, attitudes and forces playing on its formulation.

From a definition of education, action follows. Goals are given to the educational system or to that particular part of the system for which the definition is relevant. Resources of manpower and materials are claimed for education. Schools are built and teachers allocated to their staffs. As the system grows in complexity coordination becomes essential and administrators try to integrate the various parts of the system. They must, for example, control the movement of children from early schooling into the more specialized types of schools that cater for older children. Various types of administrative mechanisms have to be evolved to cope with the increasingly complicated nature of the educational system. Growth seems to lead to greater differentiation in all systems. For instance, schools or institutions of higher education become more specialized and very often this complexity in itself demands a redefinition of the system so that the legal framework, or even the conceptual framework with which people think about the system, can be brought up-to-date.

Finally, once any system has been established, steps have to be taken to ensure that the pattern into which it has been formed is maintained. Thus, in an educational system measures are needed to see that new teachers act in such a way that the goals given to the system are fulfilled. This is mainly achieved by the careful selection and training of teachers. Again, it is necessary to ensure that the products of the various levels of schools meet the requirements laid upon the system by the ruling definition. One way of achieving this is through some form of examination system.

The definitions of education that are made official by, for example, Acts of Parliament or administrative regulations do not last for ever. The sources of change may be either internal or external to the system. Change can come from outside the system in various ways. The balance of power responsible for the last truce situation may change and a new truce follow. The values governing one particular institution that inter-relates closely with education may alter with the result that it assumes greater or less importance. Thus a higher value may be put on the economy or a lower value on religion, with consequent effects for education. Or change may come from within the educational system itself; that is, the system may autonomously generate change.

This latter case is common in an atmosphere of *laissez-faire*, since any definition will tend to allow a range of tolerable action. In itself this is wise since a certain amount of tension can be permitted within the system without the necessity for constant redefinition. In concrete terms there will be no need for new Education Acts every few years. In addition, such indeterminacy in definitions allows cumulative movement within the system towards the limits of the definition, thereby influencing the direction of the next definition from within the educational system itself. Such a process is very important for the analysis of the development of English education because the educational system grew in a period when the philosophy of *laissez-faire* was strongly supported by those in power. As a result scope

3

for freedom and experiment has been usual at every level of the educational system. In such a situation minor changes can accumulate until a threshold is reached; but beyond that point a small strain may result in the need for a massive redefinition.

Briefly, then, this book will proceed by examining the way in which definitions of education have given goals to the system so that resources are drawn into the educational sector. This process leads to increasing complexity; coordination becomes more difficult, as does the problem of maintaining the existing pattern of the whole educational system. By examining the strains that lead to redefinitions and also the power struggles that result in new truce situations the sources of change that affect the educational system should be apparent. Lastly, because of the great emphasis put upon freedom in England during the last hundred and fifty years, allowance has been made in the analytical framework so that any autonomous development that may have occurred within the educational system itself can be noted and examined.

There have been three major definitions of education in England since about 1800 from which major administrative changes have flowed. These were made by and as a result of the Education Acts of 1870, 1902 and 1944. These Acts in the main refer to the schools rather than to higher, technical or further education. But very often definitions of these parts of the educational system were made at much the same time and because of much the same social strains. It will, therefore, be possible to interweave the story of these institutions with that of the schools so as to give a more complete picture of the relationship of society and education during the period.

The next chapter will study the development of the rather primitive educational system of this country in the first half of the nineteenth century and the strains that produced the 1870 Education Act. In Chapters 3 and 4 the Education Acts of 1902 and 1944 will be examined in the same way. In Chapter 5 the growth of the system since 1944 will be considered, and the strains at present at work between education and other social institutions will be examined. The recent definitions by various official reports will be described with a view to looking forward to the nature of the next redefinition. The final brief chapter will look at some of the educational and sociological generalizations that are possible as a result of using this particular conceptual framework to order the historical material presented here.

CHAPTER TWO

THE BIRTH OF THE EDUCATIONAL SYSTEM

The first attempts by the state to intervene in education in the nineteenth century were unsuccessful. Following a severe outbreak of fever in 1795 in Manchester a committee on health was established of which the first Sir Robert Peel was a member. Through his pressure in parliament the Health and Morals of Apprentices Act was passed in 1802. Factory owners were now supposed to provide adequate instruction in the three R's during the first four of the seven years of a child's apprenticeship. This schooling was not to be given before 6 a.m. nor after 9 p.m. An interesting point to note is that here education was defined as a state responsibility only inasmuch as parliament should make the rules by which it was to be supplied. The definition was not such that the state should actually supply educational facilities or levy taxation for this purpose.

The extremely simple education clauses of this Act were ineffective because of the impossibility of enforcing them at a time when the machinery of government was minimal. For the same reason the educational clauses of the 1819 Factory Act had no real success. It was not until 1833 that in a lightly attended sitting the House of Commons passed a motion to grant up to £20,000 per year to certain recognized religious societies as a subsidy for educational building and maintenance. By 1839 this sum had risen to £30,000 and it was clear that some special body was necessary to administer the grant. What constraints were working at this time to prevent more extensive state intervention in education? Why was the first successful intervention on such a comparatively small scale, and why was it restricted to the supply of monies for others to spend as opposed to the actual provision of educational facilities?

1 Constraints

At the start of the nineteenth century Britain was leading the world in industrial and commercial development. Certainly, if the rulers of this country had so wished, there was wealth enough available to allocate a larger proportion of the national income to educational purposes than was then the case. This allocation could have been made either by the state or by private citizens; more especially the wealthy could have bought more education through the almost completely *laissez-faire* economic system of the time. Yet compared with the economic system, which even in 1800 was an extremely complicated one, the educational system remained in a very simple and undeveloped state.

Though the economy was complex its smooth running did not yet depend upon the educational system for a supply of formally educated manpower, whether at the managerial or the operative level. In almost every job, except in the traditional professions of the law, medicine and the church, a man could learn by doing the job. The size of the average industrial unit was not so large as to make management a very difficult task. Many businesses were still under family ownership and there was no really strong and continuing political opposition to such nepotism. Able men who were illiterate could rise from the lower classes to the position of foreman and even into managerial positions. For the vast majority of jobs, even when skilled, a knowledge of the three R's was just not necessary. Manufacturers were proud of the skill of the British working man and spoke of the factory as the school for workmen. In general, labour was in easy supply and a demand for raw labour to learn the many new jobs created by technological change could easily be met by workers moving off the land or, especially in the mid-1840s, by Irish immigrants.

The *laissez-faire* values implicit in this view of the economic system and of the labour market were also powerful in contemporary political discourse. In 1776 Adam Smith had written *The Wealth of Nations*. This book had great influence and provided the theoretical framework within which both economic and political argument was pursued. A policy of minimum intervention was almost unquestioned by those in power, except in matters of defending the state against such external dangers as invasion or such internal threats as rebellion. Strong arguments against the provision of education by the state were based upon the claims of individual liberty in so crucial a sphere as education. Adam Smith was, however, a Scot who knew from experience that education was the basis of good civil government, of much economic activity and of social progress. Like Jeremy Bentham, a powerful *laissez-faire* theoretician of the period, he considered that state intervention might be necessary if private enterprise failed to provide what was essential for the good of the state. Therefore, when by the early nineteenth century some voices demanded more education, there was in the final resort a theoretical position to which appeal could be made. But, once it was granted that intervention was to occur, there were two very important questions to be decided. The first was who in the long run was to find the resources from which more adequate educational provision could be made and the second was what was to be taught, to whom and to what depth.

The books, including school textbooks, available to the early Victorians showed the general attitude that was adopted towards education. This reinforced many of the central political, moral and religious attitudes of the time. One of the best examples is Samuel Smiles's *Self Help*, first published in 1859. This widely read book was a series of homilies on the qualities necessary for success in life and an encouragement to all to help themselves to success by cultivating these individualistic qualities. Many of the cheap books provided earlier in the century by the upper classes for the lower classes were of a similar nature, and revealed their total lack of understanding of how the working class was really thinking at the time.

The demand for any sort of reading material was restricted in three ways. Firstly, the rate of literacy was low; in 1841,

33 per cent of men and 49 per cent of women marrying in England and Wales made their mark on the register as opposed to writing their signature.[1] Though at this time more could read than write, these figures are some measure of contemporary literacy. Secondly, political control of newspapers and magazines was an influential factor since there was a fairly heavy stamp tax on such material until as late as 1855. These taxes were originally imposed in the period just after the Napoleonic wars with the aim of checking the spread of revolutionary ideas. Yet their ultimate effect was to stir up opposition to the government. The experience of such political movements as those at the time of the Reform Bill agitation in the early 1830s and those associated with the Chartists during the years 1836 to 1848 was a very real education in itself for the illiterate millions of the working class. They learnt new aims amongst which was the demand for education, a demand based on its individual, rather than on its social, benefits.

The third restriction on the demand for reading matter was rooted in the sheer lack of leisure amongst the vast majority of the working population, tied as they were to the factory or the fields for the very long working hours of the time. Most labourers were at work by 6 a.m. and except for short meal breaks worked through until 8 p.m. It is not surprising, therefore, that in the 1850s the approximate daily circulation of newspapers was 60,000, whereas on Sundays the demand rose to about 275,000 copies.[2] Nor, in view of the education that the working class had received in the political struggles of the period after the Napoleonic wars, is it very surprising that, as soon as the tax on advertisements was removed in 1853 and the Stamp Act was repealed in 1855, seventeen provincial daily papers were founded. A substantial working-class demand was implicit in such a growth.

Each social class had a different view of what its own education should be, and the upper classes also had opinions on what

[1] J. W. Dodds, *The Age of Paradox*, London, 1953, quoted by M. Argles, *South Kensington to Robbins*, London, 1964, p. 6.

[2] For this and other figures of newspaper circulation see R. Williams, *The Long Revolution*, London, 1961, especially Chapter 2 ('The Growth of the Reading Public') and Chapter 3 ('The Growth of the Popular Press').

education the other social classes should have. These definitions of education might be implicit in their behaviour and attitudes or made explicit in public statements or in writings. Even after the Reform Act of 1832 the English aristocratic upper class was for many years a powerful group. To members of this class education for their children was not needed for any immediate practical purpose, but more to acquire social graces. This was a leisured class of rulers and their leisure was regarded by them as one important symbol of high status. Unproductive knowledge such as that of the classics or literature gave prestige in much the same way as did gaming and hunting. If this class considered the education of the other classes at all, its view was that their education, as any other commodity they needed, should be bought.

The middle class grew in size and economic importance as the country became more industrialized after the middle of the eighteenth century. This changed economic status was translated into greater political power in the reformed parliament after 1832. The upper middle class wanted to demonstrate their apparent rise in status by giving their children the same education as was normal for the upper class. They therefore imitated the educational methods of the aristocrats which then relied mainly on private tutors and on the public schools. The middle class as a whole had much the same *laissez-faire* view of the education of the working class as the upper class had of middle-class education. The one exception was that some of the middle class who lived in small country towns had come to expect a cheap or even free education at local grammar schools, most of which were heavily subsidized by endowments made in the past. The increasingly numerous lower middle class, especially in the industrial areas where their strength lay, wanted enough education for their boys for them 'to get on'. They were, therefore, keen that the curriculum of such local grammar schools as existed should consist of more utilitarian subjects like mathematics and French rather than the classical diet which was almost universal. But such a change in curriculum was not easy to achieve. In 1795 the governors of Leeds Grammar School went to the Court of Chancery to try to change the legal basis of their endowment so as to provide a more modern curriculum. But in

10

1805 Lord Chief Justice Eldon decided that these modern subjects could only be included as ancillary to the basic curriculum of the classics. He based his judgment on the definition of a grammar school found in Dr Johnson's dictionary, namely that it was a school where the learned languages are taught grammatically.

The working-class view of education was far less formed than that of the other classes. The members of this class did not question the way in which the middle and upper classes defined their own education and were only beginning to formulate their own educational needs. During the political agitations associated with Robert Owen around 1830 strong working-class support was gathered for an ideal of social justice which included a demand for popular education. This demand was also an ingredient in the Chartist movement of the period up to 1848. But it was only at the height of these movements that it can be said that there was a strong demand from the masses for education and at such times the demand was vague, not extending to the specification of the details of a curriculum.

The various religious bodies, who provided most of the formal education available for the working class, were quite explicit on what kind of education should be provided because they had a very clear goal at which to aim. Their schools were provided for religious purposes. Their aim was that the next generation should believe in the Christian religion. Children must, therefore, learn to read the Bible. The ability to write was less important than the ability to read, and some even held that it might be dangerous to teach writing since he who could write might write criticisms of the faith and of the established political order. The nature of the texts and readers used in the schools provided by the various denominations reflected these views.

The churches encouraged the view amongst the upper and middle classes that education was a worthwhile outlet for their charity. For the established Church of England this was seen as supplying education from above; the Methodists, powerful in the industrial cities, used a more democratic system of class meetings to train simple folk in the Bible. To both these religious bodies the connections between education and a stable political system was obvious. For the country as a whole, religion was at this time a key social institution and, both because of this fact and because the churches were the main providers of education, no major change was possible unless the agreement of the religious bodies was gained.

The family was another important institution. The education of girls was seen as essentially a family concern. At all levels of society girls learnt at home the vocational requirements for their future tasks as wives. In the upper and middle classes there were additional accomplishments such as singing and fine needlework that had to be learnt from governesses. Middle- and upper-class girls at this date did not look forward to careers. An education within the family was also in large measure usual for boys up to the 1830s. The resident tutor was common even if only until boys went away to school in their early teens. In these higher classes 'education' in any formal sense meant that of boys; in the working class, though girls were expected to pick up the simplest skills of housewifery, formal 'education', when considered at all, tended to apply equally to both boys and girls. At a time when many children went out to work at five years of age the main instrument of early education was still the family.

Education had not yet come to be defined as a separate discipline or subject. Many great thinkers indirectly propounded views on the topic. Those of Adam Smith have already been mentioned. Some took a Puritanical view, seeing education as part of the fight against original sin. Similarly Malthus thought that education would raise the tone of society and help to restrict the rapid rise in population. Others took a more rationalist view. Despite the lack of physical contact with the Continent during the wars with France, ideas from abroad percolated into this country. Robert Owen was the man who in his writings and in his practice did most to publicize these views. His *New View of Society*, published in 1816, stressed the way in which environment formed, and hence could reform, character. In the same year he opened an infant school at his factory at New Lanark where he translated his philosophy into practice. News of this experiment soon spread throughout Britain and abroad. It had some influence on future developments. Certainly, partly

12

as a result of Owen's work, infant education could be said to have a practice based on theory much earlier than any other branch of education in this country.

To summarize the constraints on education in England in the early nineteenth century: education was defined as the bare three R's for the working class and only free if they absolutely could not afford it. For the other classes payment was on the whole not questioned and education was still seen, particularly for girls, as a family matter, though upper- and middle-class boys were more frequently going away to school. For these classes education was not considered necessary for 'getting on', but the lower middle classes were beginning to define education as utilitarian. The educational system was not seen as essential to the economy, mainly because it was not in fact so. Nor was there yet, as on the Continent, any recognized tradition of education as a theory or as a subject for philosophical inquiry in its own right.

2 Growth

Early in the nineteenth century the public schools were described with a certain element of truth as 'the very seats and nurseries of vice'. Bullying, physical cruelty and sexual malpractices seem to have been common, and little attempt was made by staff to control such abuses. At Eton, for example, boys were locked up in a large dormitory at night and left alone with no adult interference until the door was opened for early morning school next day. However, despite the criticisms of these schools and the high standing of the family as an educational institution, there was some increase in the demand for places at the public schools in the early nineteenth century. Much of this came from the new industrial rich, who wanted to give their sons the educational stamp that they saw was necessary before their heirs could really claim the social status to which the parents aspired as a result of their new wealth. Some schools realized that reform was necessary if they were to survive. At Shrewsbury, for instance, Dr Butler, who was head from 1798 to 1836, introduced a somewhat less classical curriculum containing some English, Geography and English History,

13

and he also raised the moral tone of his school. One result was that considerable resources were poured into these schools and also into the schools which prepared boys for entry to the public schools. This was the birth of the preparatory school of today.

One of these new preparatory schools was opened at Laleham in Middlesex by the Reverend Thomas Arnold, who was to become the headmaster of Rugby School from 1828 to 1842. During his period at Rugby Arnold totally reformed that school and made it the model for the English public school of the later nineteenth century, an institution that has deeply influenced the development of the whole English educational system. Arnold's aims were to turn out Christians and gentlemen who were also, if possible, scholars. He organized the school in such a way that the older boys, his prefects, were responsible to him for the discipline of the school. He influenced the older boys in the school by taking a major part in teaching the sixth form and in this way came to know all these boys personally. In addition the school as a whole was directly under his influence because of the importance he gave to his sermons in chapel. Arnold took great care in his choice of housemasters and assistant masters so that supervision throughout the school was much more thorough than was usual in such schools at that time. The curriculum too was modified. Though Classics still formed the core, some French and Mathematics were included, as was Modern History. To Arnold History was seen as important in that it could provide models to aid in the development of character.

At the time of Arnold's death he had built Rugby into one of the most famous of the public schools. Originally it had been a small-town grammar school. Arnold was not the only strong headmaster who took over an endowed grammar school and turned it into a nationally known public school. Other examples were Repton and Uppingham. Often the headmaster established a boarding house in his own home and from this grew other houses under housemasters so that ultimately, as the country grew wealthier and the demand for education from the new upper middle class rose, the accretion to the old grammar school became the main part of the school. In these cases the grammar school meeting local needs was replaced by a few scholarship

14

places or, as at Rugby, by a new foundation for town day boys. Rather ironically one of the major industrial developments of the mid-nineteenth century helped the successful entrepreneur to send his son away to school. The spread of the railway system eased the growth of the private school system.

The rest of the middle class also wanted education. Many could not afford to send their sons away to a public school and often, particularly in the case of the lower middle class, did not want the 'useless' classical curriculum provided in such schools. There were relatively fewer endowments in the north and midlands which now had come to be the areas of rising population, since in the sixteenth and seventeenth centuries, when the majority of these schools were endowed, the weight of population was in the south. Where there were old grammar schools, they were often in sore straits. For example, Whitgift at Croydon had a large enough endowment for a master and an usher (assistant teacher), but in the early nineteenth century it was found that the master, a clergyman, took the whole endowment and appointed no usher, took no pupils but played billiards a great deal!

In this situation those who could afford it called into being the sort of educational institution that they were willing to pay for, namely fee-paying schools for day pupils with a curriculum that came much closer to meeting their own utilitarian needs. These proprietary schools, as they came to be known, were initially profit-making bodies like any other business at that time, though eventually some of them were able to gain endowments and become charitable bodies of the same legal standing as the older endowed public schools. Famous day schools of this type founded at the time were the City of London School (1837) and Liverpool College (1840). Several boarding schools, for instance Cheltenham College (1841) and Marlborough College (1843), were also set up at this time. An interesting sidelight on the claims for status of the middle class is that several of the proprietary schools established in the 1840s and 1850s were 'Colleges', in imitation of the ancient foundation of Winchester College (1382) and of the royal foundation, Eton College (1440).

Many of the proprietary schools modelled themselves on Arnold's Rugby and were soon accorded the title of public schools, though not given the same status as Eton or Winchester. The characteristic marks of the public school were clear by the middle of the century. The curriculum was predominantly classical. This was partly a historical survival. The classics were the vocational education of the intending priests who were the pupils of the pre-reformation grammar schools. However, the eighteenth-century aristocrat had also learnt the classics either at such a school or from his tutor, so that in the nineteenth century the aspiring industrialist was keen that his son should learn a non-vocational subject to put the stamp on his claim to status. Furthermore, a knowledge of the classics was essential for entry to the university, and another mark of the public schools was that they aimed to send many of their pupils on to the universities. These schools also clearly recruited mainly from the upper social strata and were for boys only. Lastly, they were much influenced by Arnold's methods. The headmaster had pastoral care of the corporate body of the school which was organized into houses and controlled with the help of prefects. The boys learnt early those lessons in taking responsibility that were needed so much as the boundaries of Empire lengthened.

All that has been said here about middle-class schools has applied mainly to those for boys only. There were very few such schools for girls. It was usual for the upper and middle class to keep their daughters at home where governesses taught them reading and writing, a little general knowledge, sometimes a smattering of French, and nearly always such accomplishments as needlework and singing. Some of the middle class sent their daughters to boarding schools. Thus the Brontës, later to become governesses, went away to a school for the daughters of the clergy and from the school described by Charlotte in *Jane Eyre* we can judge that these schools were in many respects little better than similar schools for boys. The food was bad, the discipline inhuman and the teaching poor.

The attempt to improve the educational standards of governesses that was begun by the founding of the Governesses' Benevolent Association in 1843 clearly showed the inadequacy

16

of most girls' schools, since their pupils were unable to pass the examinations inaugurated in 1846 for those intending this career. As a result, classes were begun in London at Queen's College, Harley Street. These were taught by eminent clergymen since they alone could be trusted to teach young ladies unchaperoned. Two of the early pupils of these classes were Miss Buss, who became headmistress of North London Collegiate School in 1850, and Miss Beale, who was appointed headmistress of Cheltenham Ladies' College in 1858. These were two of the schools that grew up to meet the new demand for an education for girls of a type similar to that given to their brothers. The movement for the emancipation of women was beginning. It was in 1855 that Florence Nightingale went out to the Crimea to start her long work of building up a new image of nursing as a suitable occupation for middle-class women. In many ways it was unfortunate that the middle-class schools for girls should grow up as imitations of their counterparts for boys. But supporters of female emancipation wanted to show that what boys could do girls could do equally well. So, except for the addition of dancing, music and needlework, the curriculum came to be very similar to that for boys and examinations became, if anything, more important as the main criterion of female equality.

At the start of the century there were only two universities in England, Oxford and Cambridge. This may be compared with the five that existed in Scotland. The two ancient universities were still clerical institutions and were not in general over-zealous in their pursuit of learning. Many of the undergraduates had no intention of taking a degree; a minority were poor scholars often intending to become clergymen. There were no women students at all. In 1828, as a result of mainly middle-class agitation at a time when reform was very much in the air, University College, London, was founded as a non-denominational university. In answer to what they christened 'the Godless institution of Gower Street' the Church of England helped to found King's College in the Strand. From these two colleges grew London University. At this same time in the north the great ecclesiastical see of Durham, which was growing richer as the profits of the mining industry swelled its revenues, founded

Durham University in 1833. This action was taken largely in fear of expropriation that might follow the Reform Act of 1832.

In 1858 London University was given a new charter and its degrees were declared open to all, not merely to its own students. Now external students could gain degrees; residence was no longer essential. These regulations also enabled women to sit for degrees. The courses at London were from the 1830s aimed to satisfy the needs of the middle class. Thus science, medicine and soon engineering became important departments. The B.Sc. joined the B.A. as a worthwhile degree.

In 1850 Oxford and Cambridge were the subjects of Royal Commissions as a result of which some reforms took place. Many of those in the two ancient universities came to see that they were out of touch with the changing world around them. One of the first steps that was taken to remedy this was the foundation of an examination system that would link the universities with the growing number of middle-class schools and hence with the new professional and industrial sections of society. Oxford and Cambridge established school examinations in 1857 and 1858 respectively.

Examinations had grown greatly in importance. In some measure this was part of the attack on sinecures and inefficiency that had begun with the reform of parliament. The first examinations for the Home and Indian Civil Services were held in 1855. Success in an examination was seen as a sure guarantee not only of knowledge but also of character since many Victorians thought that the latter was a prerequisite for gaining the former. The need for formal qualifications guaranteed by impartial examinations under the aegis of nationally known bodies was also implicit in the way the professions were developing. This was particularly true in the case of the medical profession. An Act in 1815 laid down that doctors had to qualify; they were to be examined and licensed by the Society of Apothecaries. This mode of qualification spread to newer professions. In 1846 the College of Preceptors was established to bring about better training of schoolmasters; this body was soon running examinations for schoolboys in much the same way as those begun at the same time by the Governesses' Benevolent Association. Yet

18

the aim of these examinations in the case of both men and women was more to ensure adequate knowledge in teachers of middle-class children than to improve the technique of teaching. Prior training in methods of teaching was not considered important at this level.

An indication of the quality of the contemporary elementary schools and their teachers may be found in two facts, typical of many that could be culled from the official reports of the 1830s and 1840s. Often factory inspectors who were checking whether employers were fulfilling the educational provisions of the Factory Acts found that certificates of attendance for pupils were signed not with the teacher's signature but with his mark, since he was unable to write. Again, in 1845 one of the first inspectors of schools found a very deaf hunchback as master of a school in Yorkshire; the explanation was that if such a man were employed as a teacher, at least the parish had no need to put him on the Poor Rate. The status of the schools for the lower classes was all too often indicated by such instances.

There were three main types of school available to the urban working class in the early nineteenth century. Firstly, there were Sunday Schools provided by the various denominations, either free or at a very nominal cost. These schools met the aims of the denominations in that they taught a minimum curriculum for religious needs and provided an outlet for charity. They did, however, meet the apparently growing thirst for knowledge of the working class on the only day of the week on which they were able to go to school. For many children Sunday was the day on which they did not go to the factory or down the mine, but instead went to church and school to gain what bare literacy was possible. Secondly, there were the dame schools. These were run by women for small fees often in very insanitary quarters such as damp cellars. Sometimes children were actually taught, but often these schools could only be described as providing a poor quality child-minding service for working mothers.

These two types of school, however, were by no means as important as the monitorial schools, which dated from the first decade of the century when Joseph Lancaster and Dr Andrew Bell had sponsored two versions of a particular method of teaching that was very much in tune with contemporary economic thought. Basically, the master taught the senior pupils, called monitors, some small piece of knowledge and they went off to teach the pupils. Monitors came and went; the master was always busy with some monitors, whilst others were teaching. Pupils were constantly at work and knowledge passed by a two-step process from master to pupil. All was rationally organized as any well-run organization should be, and the cost of operation was low.

Lancaster's system was supported by the British and Foreign School Society (1814) and Bell's by the National Society for Promoting the Education of the Poor in the Principles of the Established Church (1811). Both were religious societies; the former was interdenominational and the latter was Anglican. Large numbers of monitorial schools were founded by these societies. Their aim was to teach the bare three R's to working-class children so that they could receive the faith. In addition, girls were sometimes taught a little needlework. Obedience was the main quality of character to be inculcated, since this was seen by many as a social necessity if the growing cities were to be kept free of rebellion during and after the Napoleonic wars. Given the aims and the spirit of the times this was one possible method of channelling resources into an educational system for the masses. Furthermore, it was the first and only serious attempt at that time to evolve a method of group teaching.

Robert Owen's work in infant teaching was an important exception to this generalization. He gave advice to many, and one of his teachers went from New Lanark to London. His influence can also be seen in the methods of David Stow of Glasgow, who in 1836 published his 'Training System', a book advocating improved ways of teaching young children. More particularly Stow advocated class teaching rather than the monitorial system, which by then was the commonest method used in schools for the working class. New methods were also adopted under the influence of the famous Swiss educationalist Pestalozzi, and the Home and Colonial Society founded a training school for infant teachers on these lines in London in 1836.

Throughout the 1830s more schools were being built under the auspices of the National and the British and Foreign School societies, both of which favoured the monitorial system. Since 1833 these societies, as the only organized providers of education on any large scale, had been the recipients of the government grant of £20,000 per year that was mentioned at the start of this chapter. The government matched each pound that the societies put up with another pound. Priority was given to schools for over four hundred children. By 1839 the grant had been increased to £30,000 and the complexities of administration were such that some new arrangement was clearly necessary. Since the original grants had been made through the Privy Council, a Committee of the Privy Council was established and became the first governmental body responsible for any form of education in modern England. A secretary with a small staff was appointed. This was Dr J. P. Kay (later Sir James P. Kay-Shuttleworth) who was to become the first great English educational administrator and who deeply influenced the future development of education in this country.

Kay-Shuttleworth had visited Holland whilst a Poor Law Commissioner and seen how elementary school teachers learnt their job by undergoing a form of apprenticeship. He had briefly tried out this pupil-teacher system in a workhouse school in Norfolk. He realized that the first priority in any expansion of the English educational system was to improve the quality and supply of teachers. When he became Secretary of the Committee of Privy Council he set about this as his major task. He tried to establish a training college, or as it was then known a Normal School, but ran into opposition from the religious bodies. He was therefore forced to found one of the earliest efficient training colleges for teachers in his own house at Battersea, London, in 1840. There had been training institutions run by the societies in cathedral and other towns where teachers had gone to learn the monitorial system, but the courses were brief and adapted for monitorial schools. The course at Kay-Shuttleworth's Normal School lasted about a year, though often teachers were tempted away before completing the full course. They were taught various academic subjects as well as the methods of class teaching. His school was imitated by the National Society particularly.

Soon there were Normal Schools in several cathedral towns, financed partly by the Committee of Council.

By 1849 the government's expenditure on education had risen to £100,000. From 1833 control of money had been important in an age when business efficiency was considered crucial. Kay-Shuttleworth borrowed the idea of inspectors from the system by which the Factory Acts were administered, and in 1840 the first two H.M.I.s (Her Majesty's Inspectors) were appointed basically to see that monies granted for education were not wasted. However, as the instructions given to the early H.M.I.s by Kay-Shuttleworth show, they were seen as the eyes and ears of the Committee with the task of reporting on the social and educational circumstances of the schools and also of advising teachers on educational matters.

In 1846 Kay-Shuttleworth issued his famous Minutes on the arrangements for pupil-teachers. Able pupils of thirteen and over were to be apprenticed to teachers approved by H.M.I.s for a period of five years during which time they improved their own knowledge and practised teaching; H.M.I.s were to report on their progress. At the end of their apprenticeship they were eligible for an examination that could lead to a Queen's Scholarship available to finance training at one of the new colleges. It was recognized that some who did not gain scholarships and could find no other backing for a college course or who found that they did not want to teach would leave the schools. But Kay-Shuttleworth realized that these men would be eagerly sought as clerks in industry or commerce at a time when the school system was not organized to produce men with such middle-range qualifications. In fact, one complaint of the early colleges was that many of their qualified teachers were tempted away by higher salaries into administrative work in commerce or industry.

Kay-Shuttleworth retired in 1849, but on the basis laid down by him great expansion occurred. By 1852 the parliamentary grant on education was £160,000 and by 1859 it had risen to £836,920. The administrative task involved in this increase was vast because grants were paid direct from the Committee to individual schools. In 1856 this burden was recognized by the creation of an Education Department, and by 1857–8 there were

56 officers in addition to some 20 H.M.I.s. Yet despite this growth the Newcastle Commission that reported on the state of popular education in 1861 found that out of a child population of 2½ million only 1½ million were in school. Furthermore the size of the classes was very great. The policy of the Education Department in the late 1850s was to try to ensure that new schools were built so that one teacher had to control only 150 pupils because his assistants were at best pupil-teachers.

Many of these teachers were still untrained and their status was low. Thomas Arnold had commented that schoolmasters, as the teachers of the middle class were known, owed their status to their connection with the clergy. Many masters were clergymen and as such ranked as gentlemen in England. The teachers of the working class were rising in status as more became educated as a result of Kay-Shuttleworth's reforms, which to some extent stressed liberal education as well as teaching method. Indeed by the late fifties it was apparent that many elementary teachers were better educated than their middle-class betters. Yet their status was not that of a professional doctor or lawyer. Compared with the secondary schoolmaster, however, new recruits to the elementary schools were at least specifically trained for teaching. Many had undergone both a pupil-teachership and a period at college. Very few secondary schoolmasters were trained, mainly because headmasters did not see any necessity for this. However, there was a growing realization that if teaching was to become a profession in the fullest sense entry would have to be limited to those who were fully qualified. In 1858 the medical profession had received further legal protection and the General Medical Council was established. One of its responsibilities was to safeguard the quality of the profession by laying down entry qualifications and by keeping a register of qualified practitioners. During the sixties there was a vigorous agitation for a Teachers' Register. Despite an attempt at legislation in 1869 this movement failed mainly on the grounds that such a control of entry would interfere with the liberty of individuals.

The training of teachers for the elementary schools had developed on the lines laid down by Kay-Shuttleworth. The college that he set up at Battersea much influenced the future development of training colleges. It was residential and stressed a Christian and a corporate life. The students were seen as candidates for a vocation. Because of the inadequacy of the education of intending teachers both school subjects and methods of teaching were taught. It was usual for the college to have a model school attached where demonstrations could be given and practice take place. By 1845 there were some 22 church training colleges in England and Wales that had developed with state aid out of the earlier diocesan Normal Schools. In 1852 Kay-Shuttleworth estimated that four-fifths of the cost of a college place was supplied from government funds. There were colleges for both sexes, though none were co-educational. By 1855 the syllabuses were controlled by the Education Department as a result of regulations governing the giving of grants. This led to a common approach. Furthermore, the staff had to be qualified to impart knowledge and therefore had to have a degree. They therefore were pupils of middle-class schools and tended to be out of touch with or lacking in experience of the elementary schools. By the early sixties criticisms became common, though despite all their deficiencies these colleges were aiming to give the future teachers, and through them the working class, a more liberal and cultivated education than was usual in contemporary teachers. In addition the supply of teachers with training had risen. In 1850 there were 4,190 pupil-teachers; by 1860 the numbers had risen to 13,237.[1] Matthew Arnold, the poet and son of Thomas Arnold, was an H.M.I. and described pupil-teachers as 'the sinews of English public instruction'.

Finally, something must be said about technical instruction. It is worth noting that at this time this was the phrase used and not the more familiar 'technical education' of today. In 1800 George Birkbeck gave some classes to artisans at Anderson's Institute, Glasgow. He realized that there was a demand and a need for such introduction. Out of this experience grew the Mechanics' Institute movement. Up and down the country, particularly in the industrial areas, Mechanics' Institutes were

[1] A. Shakoor, *The Training of Teachers in England and Wales, 1900–1939,* unpublished Ph.D. thesis, University of Leicester, 1964.

built to supply classes to artisans. Originally the aim was to teach the scientific principles behind the trades that skilled men practised. But this movement was premature because these men were as yet often illiterate and usually ignorant of the first principles of mathematics, so that they were totally unable to understand the science that was taught them. By the 1830s Mechanics' Institutes had come mainly to provide the lower middle class with lectures on a great variety of topics as a leisure time activity. Furthermore the artisans of the 1830s and 1840s wanted to discuss the political and religious issues so central to the agitation of the period, but such topics were excluded from the activities of the Mechanics' Institutes.

A second and ultimately far more important source of technical instruction was created in 1853, namely the Department of Science and Art. This had been set up as a direct result of the Great Exhibition of 1851 when some percipient observers noted that the techniques and the standard of design of the Continental exhibitors was catching up on those shown by British industry. This department was established at South Kensington geographically apart from the Education Department and, though both were under the same minister, the Vice-President of the Committee of the Privy Council, the two departments pursued somewhat disparate policies.

The work of the Department of Science and Art was very difficult because there was no real demand for technical instruction. British manufacturers still felt secure in their pre-eminence. In their opinion their workshops produced the highest-quality goods in the world and this was done by the best workmen in the world who were trained in the best way possible, namely by practical experience. Factory owners had a profound distrust of the theoretical. In addition they suspected that if their employees went to classes where they met workers from other factories trade secrets would be communicated to their competitors.

Nor was there in general any supply of managers with a higher education that was in the least oriented towards industry. There were a few B.Sc.s from London, more especially in chemistry, who went into industry. It must be remembered that

c

it was only in 1840 that William Whewell, Master of Trinity College, Cambridge, coined the word 'scientist'. 'We need', he wrote, 'very much to describe a cultivator of science in general. I should incline to call him a scientist.' The older universities not only did not see the need to apply science to industry but tended to distrust the pursuit of science altogether. Mathematics was seen as an excellent training for the intellect, and many of those who then passed the Mathematics Tripos at Cambridge became judges. For these reasons the growth of technical education was even more retarded than that of the education of the working class.

Let us try to sum up briefly the state of education in England in about 1860. The goals defined for education were minimal; so, few resources were allocated to the building of an educational system. Those schools that had come into being were in large measure provided from private resources despite the increasing expenditure of the Education Department. The upper class provided its own education either within the family or at boarding schools, many of which were supplied by endowments many centuries old. The middle class was imitating its 'betters' either by patronizing the same schools or by calling into being new proprietary day or boarding schools. This system of education owed nothing to the government and was not coordinated by it. It should perhaps be stressed that the public schools did not create class divisions in England, but that the presence of these divisions strengthened the existing public school system, thereby eventually reinforcing the already existing class system of this country.

The schools for the working class were seen as something apart. Since the lower classes were unable to create 'popular' schools for themselves the 'elementary' schools that were created for them were first of all given in charity. Later in a *laissez-faire* system cheapness came to be the governing spirit; little was to be spent and that with care. There were comparatively few who like Kay-Shuttleworth planned in a humane way. His work was beginning to have an effect. More especially the supply of teachers was improving in quantity and quality. This had its influence on the standard of schooling and in a broader curriculum. However, by the late 1850s the success of Kay-Shuttleworth's measures and of the organization that he had created to further the education of the working class was one of the main reasons why the truce situation of the early nineteenth century broke down and why the first major state definition of education was to take place in the 1860s. Before turning to this, however, the strains that led to a breakdown of the old definition must be considered.

3 Strains

The new Education Department was an autonomous force within the system of government. The more money the societies found, the more the government had to produce from its revenue for educational purposes. The rapid increase in expenditure by the Education Department took place in a decade that was to close with a government in power dedicated to reducing expenditure at home and abroad. Gladstone was the Chancellor of the Exchequer. His aim was to prune back all unnecessary expenditure. What must be spent must be controlled carefully. The new Education Department did not seem to fit the general pattern.

Throughout the 1850s there were attempts to pass legislation that would define the position of education more exactly. Some of these were sponsored by northern Members of Parliament representing constituencies where employers were coming to see a need for education on economic grounds, namely that only by ensuring a literate work force could Britain meet increasing foreign competition, more particularly that of Germany and the United States. None of these Bills reached the statute book, but this legislative activity did help to make explicit the problems of state action in the field of education. It soon became clear that the main obstacle to establishing an educational system provided by the state was to be found in the central position at this time of religious institutions.

The religious denominations were the main suppliers of education for the working class and the argument about the desirability of state provision did not yet on the whole extend beyond this class. Furthermore, the approach to education had

27

traditionally been in religious terms. It was, therefore, almost inevitable that any fresh consideration of the problem of education for the poor would be couched in religious terms. Fundamentally the problem was that religion was felt to be a vital element in the curriculum. Thus the denominations believed that any schools set up by the state must teach religion, but the taxpayers who would finance such a system would come from various denominations, none of which was willing to subsidize through taxation the other's brand of Christianity. A battle therefore developed between the denominations as to what kind of religion should be taught, and also between denominationalists and secularists, some of whom were quite willing to accept state aid without religious instruction, and others again who resisted the whole idea of state aid. During the 1860s the situation became very complicated with the supporters of the various groups pulling in different directions, but by the late sixties there were two main pressure groups, both of which had their supporters in parliament. There was the National Education League whose policy was that there should be publicly provided schools with no sectarian teaching, and there was the National Education Union which wanted schools providing denominational instruction. The best summary of this situation is to be found in a cartoon in *Punch* in which a group of clerical schoolmasters stand in argument before a school thereby preventing the children from entering the building at all. Basically the ironic position was that the main providers of education now blocked the further expansion that other parts of society had at last come to see as a necessity.

The greatest change of view had taken place in two of the other institutions that were relevant to education. These were the economic and the political institutions. Further international exhibitions followed the Great Exhibition of 1851. In 1867 there was an exhibition in Paris at which the rate of industrial progress of Germany in particular, but also of other industrializing countries, was very clear for all to see. Various official reports had made it clear that the rapid progress of German industry was based on a very well-organized system of state elementary schools. Observers also commented on the extremely well-disciplined nature of the German labour force, and this was at least partly attributed to the sound system of basic schooling.

These were manifest factors, but certain latent economic strains were present that worked towards the need for a new definition of education. Several industries introduced technical improvements that lowered the demand for child labour. For instance, steam was introduced into the lace and pottery industries, and the techniques in agriculture were changing. Thus these industries, formerly large employers of child labour, came to rely somewhat less on children. Each succeeding Factory Act made more difficult the employment of child labour, whether full-time or as half-timers. The economy was no longer so dependent upon the supply of child labour. By the 1860s what was worrying many was that a very large proportion of children were neither at school nor at work. Thus in Manchester in 1865 of those between the ages of three and twelve 6 per cent were at work, 40 per cent at school and 54 per cent were neither at work nor at school.[1] Economic changes seemed to be making an existing social problem even worse.

In several industries the new processes not only altered the demand for unskilled child labour, but also created a new need for highly educated scientific labour. Two instances of this process may be cited, namely the introduction of the Bessemer process into the steel industry from 1856 onwards and, a little later, the use of new dyestuffs by the cotton industry. Innovation of this nature created a demand for a new grade of labour akin to what we now know as the technician. Also the growing size of companies led to greater complexity of administration and hence to a need for clerical staff, both of the routine and non-routine categories. The introduction of limited liability by the Company Acts of 1857 and 1862 gave additional impetus to this process. The City of London had now become the centre of the world capital market and so short was the supply of clerical labour, particularly with a knowledge of foreign languages, that commercial undertakings began to recruit German and French clerks to fill the gap left by our own educational system.

These economic reasons for educational reform were reinforced

[1] F. Musgrove, *Youth and the Social Order*, London, 1964, p. 76.

by political factors. The ruling class was coming to see that a further Reform Bill must soon be passed. The 1832 Act had not gone as far as the working class had hoped since neither they nor, indeed, the whole of the middle class had been enfranchised. There was constant unsuccessful agitation throughout the thirties and forties for universal male suffrage. The good trade of the fifties seemed to reduce the pressure for the vote, but the early sixties saw much trade union activity. It was apparent to many that once the working class had the vote some system of education was essential if only to ensure a democratic consensus. Robert Lowe, a prominent Liberal Member of Parliament who was Vice-President of the Committee of Council in the early 1860s, said, 'I believe it will be absolutely necessary to compel our future masters to learn their letters.' Yet this did not mean that state provision was inevitable. There were several ways in which an educational system could be established without the central government stepping in to undertake the task. Local bodies could do so as in Prussia or the United States. State provision could continue merely to finance buildings and make grants to existing schools, and there was no reason why the salaries of the teachers might not be at least partially covered by fees.

It was legislation on education that was inevitable, not state provision. During the 1860s it became clear that the size of the task that was essential was beyond the resources of the various denominational societies and that some form of rate aid was inevitable. The new government of 1866 was known to favour the widening of the franchise. In fact, Disraeli's Reform Act of 1867 gave the vote to about half the urban working class, and they promptly voted into power the Liberals who had undertaken to initiate some action on education. The political task was in a way made more difficult by the Reform Act, since one result was that the ranks from which the main body of nonconformists came were given the vote and hence now had more power to fight the established church. In this political setting Forster introduced his Elementary Education Act of 1870.

Though clearly legislation on education was coming, its content would be governed by the current definitions of education. No one considered that the education of the upper and middle classes should be provided by the state. Therefore more attention will be given here to the definitions of education for the working class by this class itself and by the other social classes. The upper and middle classes saw that more was being spent on education and this went against the prevailing political belief in *laissez-faire*. Furthermore, they had begun to appreciate that the educational system was now acting as a selection mechanism since it provided a subsidized avenue for upward social mobility from the working to the middle class. Able working-class children of both sexes could become pupil-teachers, win a Queen's scholarship and gain middle, or at least lower, middle class status. They did this through a free education mainly financed out of taxation paid by the middle class, who were not slow to point out that they had to pay fees for the education of their own children.

As a representative of the teachers said in 1859 before the Newcastle Commission which was investigating the education of the working class, 'The Government, by assisting us to larger incomes and to better educations, has done very much to elevate our position, and we are thankful; still we conceive ourselves not holding that place in public estimation we may justly expect to hold.'[1] Though the teachers might not think their status yet high enough, many of the upper and middle classes noted that this new semi-profession was rising in numbers more rapidly than the old professions such as medicine or law or the ministry. This change in social position was being financed for the teachers by the upper classes at the very time when increased pressure was being put on the wealthier section of the community to give their own sons a longer and hence more expensive education. The reform of the Civil Service by which entry gradually came to be restricted to those who passed examinations has already been mentioned; a similar development was the establishment of the General Medical Council which also had specific implications for the examinations needed to qualify for the medical profession. Parallel changes were occurring in the legal profession and candidates for commissions

[1] *Report of Royal Commission on the State of Popular Education*, 1861, Vol. V, p. 400.

now entered officer schools only after passing a qualifying examination. The professional classes had to face a changed view of education. Similarly the changes of technique in industry on the whole led to the need for a managerial labour force with a more formal scientific education. Thus the industrial middle class was also coming to see a need to redefine their view of education and to provide more of it for themselves, if necessary by reducing what was available to the working class.

How did this lower class define its own educational needs? There was no real corporate view on education as yet, though some of the leaders of the new trade unions that recruited the skilled aristocracy of labour were starting to formulate their views. Robert Applegarth, Secretary of the Amalgamated Society of Carpenters and Joiners, gave evidence on this matter before the Royal Commission on Trade Unions in 1868. He thought that much of the contemporary industrial conflict between employer and employee was caused by sheer ignorance and that education was the answer (Karl Marx, who was writing *Das Kapital* in the British Museum at this very time, suggested a very different answer). These moderate leaders of the working class were very conscious that to gain benefits for their members, and ultimately for the working class as a whole, they must appear respectable. Their views on education were tempered by this policy and were of a very general character. They rarely discussed what was actually to be taught. Thus the working class and its movements had little direct effect on the shaping of the next definition of their own education. But because of the informal education in political activity that had drawn attention to the needs of the working class, the first Education Act that was passed in 1870 possibly went further in its provision than might otherwise have been the case.

In brief, the working class was coming to express a demand for 'education' without being too clear about what this meant in specific terms. At the same time the ruling class was coming to see a need for at least a minimum of learning for those whom they ruled and who were coming to have more political power. For themselves the upper classes were under great pressure to use the schools that could now provide a somewhat better education, though these still were far from meeting the growing scientific demands of industry.

Certainly the family was less capable now of meeting the new educational needs. The middle-class parent came to have less real knowledge about the kind of education which his sons, and to some extent his daughters, would need for their future careers. A sign of this anxiety about the future employment of their offspring may be found in the publication throughout the nineteenth century of vocational guides, handbooks for the trades and professions. The increasing provision of schools for the lower classes also had the effect of moving their formal education out of the family. Such education had certain unforeseen effects. Much modern discussion of the influence of this rise in educational provision on the working class has been carried on in terms of 'the gentling of the working class'. In other words the new schools influenced the development of their personality as well as their intellect.

As the educative function of the family declined, so that of the teacher grew more important. Some measure of this can be found in the fact that by 1868 the percentage of the undergraduates at Oxford and Cambridge who had been taught by private tutors at home rather than at schools, though still considerable, was much smaller than fifty years before. It now stood at only 11·6 per cent.[1] The family was coming to be more of an affectional base from which its members could move out into life. It still played an important part in the informal education of the young. The wealthy went on holiday *en famille* and the poor took their day outings as families. A new demand for mass leisure activities began in this era; for example, the Football Association was founded in 1863. But in all matters of formal education it was the opinion of those teaching in the schools that won the day.

4 Redefinition

There were many strains working towards a redefinition of the educational situation. The first of the new definitions came

[1] *Schools Inquiry Commission*, 1868, Vol. I, Appx VII.

around 1850 when the position of the universities was made clear. But the threshold of redefinition in the other educational fields was not reached till the 1860s, mainly under the economic and political pressures described above.

Between 1850 and 1852 both Oxford and Cambridge had been persuaded to allow Royal Commissions to investigate them. The two ancient universities were very unwilling to submit to what they considered an indignity. The recommendations of the resulting reports did not aim to bring these universities into the national system of education, but to abolish the anachronistic statutes that hindered open competition for their scholarships, the creation of new chairs and the introduction of new subjects. The Oxford University Act of 1854 and the Cambridge University Act of 1856 allowed these changes to take place though they occurred very slowly.

The year 1851 saw a major innovation in the field of higher education. As a result of a legacy from a wealthy merchant, Owens College, Manchester, was established. This was the forerunner of the civic universities that were from the 1870s to become more common in provincial English cities. These new bodies were to take their cue from Owens College in that from the very start they aimed to meet the needs of local industry. London University had defined its purpose as professional; Owens College saw itself as being to a large degree industrial. This was a very new definition of a university education that began to lay emphasis on the social, rather than the individual, functions of higher education.

During this same period the Department of Science and Art was struggling to impose its idea of technical instruction on the economic system, but with very little effect. However, the 1867 Paris Exhibition caused enough trepidation for parliament to appoint a Select Committee on Technical Instruction under a well-known ironmaster, Bernhard Samuelson. His committee reported in 1868, but rather unexpectedly its stress was as much on the provision of technical instruction for managers and foremen as on that for the lower levels of the labour force whose real need was seen to be a sound basic education, although the committee did recommend that this should have a simple

34

scientific content. This committee took the view that technical instruction should be defined as the teaching of the principles underlying techniques and not the teaching of actual practice. One witness deployed an argument that shows very clearly the way in which the *laissez-faire* ideology was central to all considerations of education. He was in favour of instruction only in the principles of the various trades because to provide teaching in the practice of any one industry would be a form of subsidy to that industry and as such was anathema to any businessman at that time. This report had no immediate effect on legislation mainly because of the very strong belief of British industry in its own superiority, but it did lead to a Royal Commission under the Duke of Devonshire which sat from 1870 to 1875 and produced an even fuller Report, though legislation was not enacted till the 1880s after a third and final inquiry by a Royal Commission with Samuelson as chairman.

In the field of school education redefinitions were not so long delayed and led to more immediate effect. As a result of the report in 1861 of the Newcastle Commission on popular education one important and far-reaching decision had already been taken. The report commented that 'The teachers sent out from the training colleges are quite good enough. . . . The object is to find some constant and stringent motive to induce them to do that part of their duty which is at once most unpleasant and most important.'[1] The Commissioners were referring to the teaching of the less able children whom they considered from their interpretation of the evidence presented to them to suffer because the teachers gave overmuch attention to their more able pupils.

The Commissioners held the common view of the period that the notion of accountability, so vital to a well-run business, should be applied vigorously to all forms of government expenditure. There was a precedent in the practice of the Department of Science and Art during the late 1850s for payment of grants in aid of education that varied according to the number of pupils who passed an examination. Payment by results was as congenial to the 1860s as the monitorial system had been to

[1] *Royal Commission on the State of Popular Education*, 1861, Vol. I, p. 157.

those allocating monies to education half a century before. The problem was translated into the administrative one of prescribing the educational standards to be achieved by children of various age levels and of organizing a yearly examination of schools to discover the number of children who passed whatever test was devised. Teachers could then be paid yearly on the actual attendances of the children in their schools or classes, but also on the measure of their efficiency, namely on the number of these children passing the specified standards.

The Newcastle Commission defined elementary education in terms of the ability to read 'a common narrative', writing 'a letter that shall be both legible and intelligible' and knowing 'enough of ciphering to make out, or test the correctness of a common shop bill' together with a little geography and the ability 'to follow the allusions and the arguments of a plain Saxon sermon' – in other words a Christian version of the three R's for boys and girls up to the age of ten or twelve.[1] This definition of the curriculum had to be translated into administrative action that met the needs of a business age.

In 1862 after much opposition from some educationalists, amongst whom Matthew Arnold was the most vociferous, the government introduced the Revised Code, a revision of the code upon which grants to elementary schools would be paid. This laid down the requirements necessary to pass at each standard (hence the name given to each class became a 'standard') and gave details of the way in which H.M.I.s were to examine schools so as to decide the grant to be paid. Robert Lowe, then Vice-President of the Committee of Council, described the new system to the House in the following way, 'If it is not cheap, it shall be efficient; if it is not efficient, it shall be cheap.' He was right; the grant to elementary schools fell from £813,441 in 1861 to £636,806 in 1865. There was a similarly depressing effect on the training colleges. Numbers of students in colleges dropped from 2,972 in 1862 to 2,403 in 1868. The recruitment of pupil-teachers also fell and two colleges were forced to close. Furthermore, changes were made in the methods by which grants were paid. Before the Revised Code payments were made direct to

[1] Op. cit., p. 243.

teachers who could be seen in some sense as state employees. After 1862 payment was made to school managers with whom teachers now had to bargain as to their rate of remuneration. Hence the status of teachers seemed lower and, in fact, their salaries did drop somewhat in the early years of the new Code.

The Revised Code certainly did much to redefine the role and the position of the teacher, the nature of the curriculum and the general standing of the elementary school. No arrangements were made to provide more schools. However, by the end of the decade Gladstone's government was pledged to take some action on this problem. A compromise was necessary that suited the various religious interests. Gladstone's Vice-President was W. E. Forster and his Elementary Education Act was passed in 1870. The object of this Act as he stated it to the House was 'to complete the present voluntary system, to fill up the gaps, sparing the public money where it can be done without . . .' Here for the first time was an administrative definition of educational provision in this country and the influence of this decision is strong to this day. The religious denominations should be allowed to go on providing schools as before and should be given the chance to fill in what gaps in provision still existed. Where they were unable to do this, the state should step in through locally elected *ad hoc* agencies, the School Boards. These bodies were to provide state elementary schools from local rate aid, providing non-denominational religious instruction where this was demanded and as long as local religious bodies agreed to the syllabus. Where parents wished they had the right to withdraw their children from religious instruction in any schools. The rest of the curriculum taught was to be controlled by the Revised Code and hence the 1870 Act took the existing mechanism for controlling the curriculum into its definition. Since the Education Department was able to change the code whenever it so desired there was unsuspected tolerance for redefinition to occur. In fact, the first slight retreat from the initial rigour of the Revised Code had already occurred in 1867.

The problem of the education of the other social classes had also to be faced, mainly because of the economic strains that had become obvious. Two Royal Commissions were appointed to investigate upper- and middle-class schools. The Clarendon Commission which reported in 1864 considered the nine major public schools – Eton, Winchester, Westminster, Harrow, Rugby, Charterhouse, Shrewsbury, Merchant Taylors' and St Paul's. The Taunton Commission sat from 1864 till 1868 and produced a report of twenty volumes on the schools that neither the Newcastle nor the Clarendon Commission had considered. *The Economist* called it 'the middle class schools commission'. It is interesting to note that the full titles[1] of neither report contained the word 'secondary'. Matthew Arnold, who had examined schools on the Continent for the Newcastle Commission, was strongly pressing that we 'organize our secondary education'. The first use of this word in its educational sense seems to have been by Condorcet in 1792 when he instituted the reorganization of French education. But 'secondary' in any educational sense was only now passing into the English language.

In the report of the Clarendon Commission the upper class defined its own education in terms of a mainly classical diet, but wished to add some mathematics and science.[2] The only recommendations that had legislative effect were those on the government of these ancient endowments. Some changes to make their administration more suited to contemporary conditions were contained in the Public Schools Act of 1868. At this level education was defined in terms of boys only. The Taunton Commission's Report was the first which contained a plan for the organization of what today would be called secondary education, and which also put stress on the secondary education of girls. Both Miss Buss and Miss Beale gave evidence to the Commission. That women should do so was commented on, but it was nevertheless a sign of how far the process of the emancipation of women had gone.

The Report of this Commission was very much influenced by the contemporary view of the social class structure and by the the needs of the economy. Three grades of school were suggested. The first was for the children of the upper and professional

---

[1] See next two footnotes.

[2] *Royal Commission on the Revenues and Management of Certain Colleges and Schools*, 1864.

classes and would continue to the age of about eighteen; it was seen as giving 'something more than classics and mathematics'. The second grade schools stopped at sixteen and were mainly to serve the mercantile and higher commercial classes. Their curriculum was, therefore, seen as containing 'a certain amount of thorough knowledge of those subjects which can be turned to practical use in business'; Latin was barely tolerated by this class of people. The third grade schools were for the upper working class ('The smaller tenant farmers, the small tradesmen, the superior artisans') and their needs were described as 'very good reading, very good writing, very good arithmetic'.[1]

Forster proposed relevant legislation in 1869 by which a substantial measure of state intervention would have become possible. Many of the public schools took fright and under the leadership of Thring, the headmaster of Uppingham, formed the Headmasters' Conference to organize opposition to the Endowed Schools Bill. However, a version of this Bill became law and enacted that a reshaped Charity Commission was to reorganize educational and some other endowments to make the most efficient use of the available resources for secondary education of both boys and girls in all parts of the country. By 1873 over three hundred new schemes had been drawn up, nearly one hundred of which had been before parliament. Such drive caused resentment and Disraeli's Conservative government passed an Amending Act which slowed down, but by no means checked, the process. There was a tendency for these schemes of reorganization to direct monies from the provision of working-class education to the establishment of new secondary schools for the middle class.

One way had been opened up for the ampler provision of middle-class education and this was to be for both boys and girls. The curriculum was seen now as having some necessary relationship to the economic system. Yet, the impact of the prevalent ethos of *laissez-faire* was considerable in the Act of 1869. Intervention in the schools that then existed was minimal and the expansion of secondary education was not to be paid for by the state but was to be financed by the reallocation of

[1] *Schools Inquiry Commission*, 1868, Vol. I, pp. 15–21.

existing endowments. The redefinition of both secondary and elementary education was made in the same spirit as that by which the businesses of the times were run, namely in terms of financial solvency, success and accountability.

5 Conclusion

By 1870 goals had been given to an elementary system which was dual in nature, since both the state and the religious denominations took a share in providing the schools. The curriculum to be taught had been defined as a summary version of the three R's for both boys and girls. These schools were very much working-class schools, very much supplied from above. They were not 'popular' schools inspired by the people for whom they were intended. The word 'elementary' came to have strong social class connotations, meaning a minimal education provided as cheaply as possible for those who could not afford better.

However, the state had at last admitted the need to provide at least part of the education of the working class. It had itself begun to provide schools, whereas up to 1870 what had been done, and much of real value had been achieved, was the result of the efforts of the denominations indirectly supported by the state. By 1869 they had provided some 1·7 million places for the 2·5 million children in the country, though the average attendance over the year was only about 1·1 million children. This positive decision by the state to intervene led to huge claims for resources as gaps in provision were filled and the minimum school-leaving age of twelve was made compulsory. Direct intervention was not the solution applied to secondary education except inasmuch as existing endowments were to be re-allocated. The middle class was to be responsible for providing the improved education that the economy demanded, in the main out of its own resources. It might be encouraged to do so, but attempts to intervene, if pushed too far, were clearly resisted. Secondary education was not yet defined as a national responsibility though it was a national need.

Though expansion was demanded and forthcoming at differing rates in all the sectors of education there was no real coordination of the various parts of the system. The Department of

Science and Art at South Kensington was increasingly out of step with elementary education, which was controlled by the Education Department from Whitehall. Both were ostensibly responsible to the same minister in parliament, the Vice-President of the Committee of Council, but the two departments proceeded along independent lines. If the secondary schools were the responsibility of anyone it was the Charity Commission, basically a legal rather than an educational body. The universities were almost independent, though their own developing sense of social need had resulted in a link with the middle-class schools through the newly established examination boards.

This ill-coordinated system was growing, but its curriculum had only recently been defined so that it in any way matched the needs of the economy, now challenged by foreign competition. This new definition did not, however, match the demands of aspirants for higher social status; at every level of the social system they demanded an imitation of the literary curriculum traditionally associated with the leisured class. The new wealthy classes wanted to buy this from the public schools or the recently founded proprietary schools, whilst in the elementary schools parents encouraged their children towards a curriculum without science or handwork. Such subjects were connected with industry and they wanted their children to be clerks or teachers. This latter profession was already a recognized avenue for moving up the social ladder and the elementary school teachers who had arrived through success in a non-scientific curriculum naturally stressed its importance to their own abler pupils. Forces internal to the schools seemed to strengthen the forces that were already at work on parents from outside the educational system. Thus, links between education and the economy were tenuous and slow to grow.

CHAPTER THREE

TOWARDS ONE SYSTEM

During the 1860s the major parts of the educational system had been defined or redefined and we must now trace their development along the lines laid down by the truce situations of that period. Though a sociologist can talk of mid-Victorian England having 'an educational system', no contemporary administrator could have spoken in this way. There were a number of very different organizations which had authority in each sector of the educational system, but there was very little coordination between these bodies. However, by passing the 1870 Act the decision was finally taken that the state itself should play a major part in the provision of education, certainly at the elementary level.

The state was also providing most of what little technical instruction there was in Britain at that time. Though both elementary and technical instruction were now, as Bentham would have said, on the state's agenda and in some sense under parliamentary surveillance, the two departments concerned made little attempt to cooperate in what they did. Debates in parliament on educational matters were rare in the 1870s and hence those in charge of the state sector of education were in a position to interpret the definitions laid down earlier with a certain freedom. The result was that they could in large measure shape the way these educational sectors developed.

Secondary education was on the whole defined as being outside the field of state intervention. The *laissez-faire* system had clearly failed to supply the elementary and technical education that was needed by the political and economic institutions of the period, so intervention was deemed essential. But despite the failure to organize an adequate provision at secondary level the truce situation arrived at would only permit the judiciary to intervene to reorganize the endowments already given to education. Once these resources were reallocated the *laissez-faire* system was to take over again. Middle-class citizens would be able to buy secondary education for their sons and daughters in just the same way as the professional and upper middle classes were now buying education for their sons from the public and proprietary schools. These schools now had a link through the examination system with the universities, a sector of education that was almost entirely unaffected by any form of state intervention. Royal Commissions that led to Acts of Parliament might force the modernization of university administration, but beyond that what went on in universities was in the absolute control of the universities themselves.

This system of education grew over the next twenty or so years in such a way that the strains implicit in the lack of coordination present in 1870 became more obvious. The possibility for autonomous development inherent in the lack of central control allowed growth in totally unintended directions. These strains were purely educational and internal to the educational system itself. In addition, as strains between education and such other factors as the economy and the political system grew more serious, conditions became ripe for the massive redefinition that took place around the turn of the century. This was to be the first attempt to construct an educational system of a unitary character in modern England.

1 Growth

In August 1870 after twenty-eight days of debate the Education Act was passed. The School Boards when elected were able to spend up to threepence in the pound of rateable value on elementary education. Though eventually devious ways were found of giving more aid to the denominations, initially they had

43

to continue to finance their existing schools and to raise the additional money to fill as many of the gaps in provision as they could. The response of the denominations was remarkable. In the decade leading up to 1880 the number of voluntary (denominational) schools rose from 8,000 to 14,000, and the number of children in these schools increased from 1·2 to 2·0 millions.[1] During this same decade the state system of elementary schools was begun, and by 1880 there were more than 3,000 such schools containing three-quarters of a million children.

Under the Act, School Boards could provide purely secular elementary schooling and in a few places this was done, but the vast majority of Boards followed the example of Manchester, where representatives of local denominations agreed to a syllabus for religious instruction, and this policy was adopted elsewhere. Such syllabuses often had all the marks of compromise and came to be called, in rather a derogatory fashion, 'School Board religion'. Areas that were predominantly nonconformist tended to have simpler and less detailed syllabuses than was the case where Anglicans were strong. The pace-setter among School Boards was the London Board, which was established by a special Act of Parliament since the problems in London were considered unique. Celebrated men such as Thomas Huxley, the scientist, and Sidney Webb, an early member of the Fabian Society, did not think themselves above standing for election and taking part in the work of this Board. London was soon in the forefront, for instance, in its methods of training pupil-teachers and in its architectural designs for schools.

It was not only the denominations but the state that had problems in raising finance to support the growth of educational provision. In 1870 Forster had stated as a policy that the cost of financing state elementary schools should be divided proportionally between fees, local funds and the Treasury so that each interest bore one-third of the total cost. However, in 1891 fees were abolished as it was realized that much hardship was involved in the poor paying even the small amounts involved ('school pence'). This abolition, which applied to both Board

[1] M. Cruickshank, *Church and State in English Education*, London, 1963, pp. 44–5.

and Voluntary schools, increased the need for grants from the Treasury to the Boards, so that by 1898 40·6 per cent of finance came from government grants, 56·6 per cent from local rates and of the remainder only 1·0 per cent was supplied by fees of various sorts. This added burden on the ratepayer can be seen in another way; in 1872 the average sum raised per scholar was 10s. 0¾d., but by 1896 it had risen to 21s. 2d.[1] From the point of view of the Treasury there were also problems because of the method by which expenditure was authorized. Once the Committee of Privy Council, which was still the body controlling expenditure on elementary and technical education, had set out in its code the types of courses that it would back with grants, there was no means of foretelling accurately the exact number of courses that any School Board would teach and hence how much payment must be made. Therefore the Treasury became increasingly aware of the need for effective financial control.

The burden of finding finance grew as the proportion of the country's children in the schools rose. The 1870 Act did not enforce compulsory education, but enacted that this was at the discretion of School Boards. By 1876 about half the population was under compulsion. The proportion was about four-fifths in urban areas where the School Boards had greater control of education than in the rural areas. In the country the denominations, more especially the Church of England, continued to supply schools in much the same way that they had done prior to 1870. In 1876 the Vice-President of the Committee of Council, Lord Sandon, introduced an Act by which attendance was made compulsory up to the age of ten and between ten and thirteen for those without a certificate showing that they had attained a certain standard in the three R's. This Act also enabled School Boards to establish School Attendance Committees to enforce attendance, though once again action was based on local committees and hence enforcement depended very much on local opinion. A few millowners and landowners were still anxious not to lose the cheapest part of their labour force. In 1880 the Vice-President, Mundella, persuaded parliament to enact that

[1] P. H. J. H. Gosden, *The Development of Educational Administration in England and Wales*, Oxford, 1966, pp. 146–7.

attendance was to be compulsory, though at eleven employment in factories was still possible. This gradual closing of the loopholes by which children left the schools at an early age meant that by 1893-4 some three-quarters of twelve- to thirteen-yearolds were still at school.

The effect of the expansion of the elementary schools on the rate of illiteracy was great. Whereas in 1871 the percentage of persons signing the marriage register with a mark was 19·4 for men and 26·8 for women, the percentage had decreased to as little as 6·4 and 7·3 by 1891.[1] A reflection of this greater literacy is found in the growth of the demand for newspapers. The rise of the provincial press took place during the period 1870–90 and of the evening press from 1880. Soon after 1900 there was a majority reading public for Sunday papers; hours of work on weekdays still militated against the growth of the dailies. It was also during the 1880s that large advertisements began to appear in the newspapers; initially these were aimed at the wealthier middle class, but soon manufacturers and distributors saw the possibility of profits implicit in appeals to a literate mass market.[2]

The curriculum taught in the elementary schools was controlled by the various successors to the Revised Code of 1862. This Code laid down just what subjects qualified for grant and the various standards to be achieved by each age level. The extreme rigour of the Revised Code was gradually relaxed under administrative changes generated within the Education Department. One of Mundella's major innovations was the establishment of a Code Committee which consisted mainly of H.M.Is. By the 1880s the Code divided the elementary curriculum into two parts. These were the obligatory subjects, namely the three R's, and optional subjects of two types. There were, firstly, what were called class subjects which could be taken throughout the school above Standard I; geography, history and plain needlework were examples. Assessment for grant for these class subjects was made not on the work of individual pupils but on the work of the class as a whole. Secondly, there were 'specific

---

[1] G. Balfour, *The Educational Systems of Great Britain and Ireland* London, 1898, p. 305.   [2] R. Williams, op. cit.

subjects, such as science, which could only be taken above Standard IV. In this way the curriculum of the elementary school began to be somewhat less narrow.

The work involved in assessment for grant had increased both because of the increased number of pupils and because of the greater complexity of administering this more liberal code. The number of H.M.I.s grew from 76 in 1870 to 352 by 1899. Teachers were often critical of H.M.I.s because they were for the most part graduates of Oxford or Cambridge and had little or no initial practical knowledge of elementary schools. Certainly it is hard to know from where else men capable of this difficult job could have been recruited in the early years of expansion, since there was still opposition to the employment of elementary school teachers as H.M.I.s. Furthermore, the H.M.I.s were strong opponents of the old and narrow Revised Code, the effect of which was felt very severely by the schools. Teachers tended to drill children to ensure that they could cope with the requirements for grant purpose at each Standard level. If they did not do this, they earned less grant for their school and, hence, ultimately for themselves. The results of the yearly inspection were vital for teachers and school alike. Teaching methods and material were therefore aimed towards passing an examination of a very limited nature. Relationships with inspectors and with children were the more difficult because of the system. Payment by results indeed merited its name and had a very deep, lasting and narrowing effect.

The Revised Code also had a drastic effect on the training of teachers. The curriculum of colleges was narrowed; this had a particularly adverse impact on the teaching of science, a subject only in its infancy in the colleges at the time. Numbers of pupil-teachers initially fell, though the 1870 Act resulted in a rapid rise in the demand. Numbers of pupil-teachers rose from 14,612 in 1870 to 34,109 in 1897. Many of these future teachers were not trained well, but were used almost as 'sweated labour'. A departmental committee considered the system in 1896–8 and on the whole still favoured it as the way to train elementary teachers. There were several grades of qualification by the turn of the century and very few teachers went or had been to a

47

training college. The output of the colleges was about 2,800 per year in 1902. Of the 10,128 who qualified for admission in 1901 only 2,732 were accommodated. Although not all these applicants may have really wished to go, the shortfall of places is staggering. In 1902 about three-quarters of the teachers serving in Voluntary or School Board schools were still untrained.[1]

One of the most remarkable of the autonomous developments that occurred in English education during this period was the probing forward by the elementary system into the older age groups that were normally considered beyond its defined limits. Various arrangements were made so that what is now known as secondary education was given within schools that were for grant purposes on the elementary code. This development may be traced to the introduction of 'specific' subjects in 1867 when the Code of 1862 was revised for the first time. These subjects were taught in special higher classes or, increasingly often, in Higher Grade Schools. The first such school was opened in 1875 in Bradford, and Higher Grade Schools were especially popular in the midland and northern industrial areas, where there was a growing demand for their pupils as clerks and technicians in commerce and industry.

A parallel development was the growth of Organized Science Schools. These schools were recognized in 1872 by the Department of Science and Art and the conditions of grant were such that more than half of the time had to be spent on scientific subjects; much of the remainder could be given over to manual work, extra mathematics or art as applied to industry. Six hours per week were left for English, languages or other subjects. By the mid-nineties strong expressions of opinion had forced these schools to teach at least ten hours of literary subjects. However, particularly after the mid-eighties there was a rapid growth in the numbers of Organized Science Schools.

What was striking about this development was that the Department of Science and Art sponsored it. This department had been established originally to provide education for the industrial classes in the scientific principles underlying industry and in art as applied to industry. By the mid-eighties its main

[1] See A. Shakoor, op. cit., pp. 112–13.

48

effort and a growing proportion of its expenditure was going towards expanding secondary education for the lower middle and upper working classes. This was a remarkable autonomous development, a redefinition of the aim of this sector of the educational system that had been made within the Department itself mainly under the inspiration of its head, Donnelly. The result was that the Department of Science and Art not only changed its own goal, but invaded the territory of its co-department, the Education Department. Both these departments were supposedly responsible to the same minister, the Vice-President, and by the mid-eighties both were exceeding their remits with his knowledge but without any real coordination.

Both the Organized Science Schools and Higher Grade Schools had grown popular by the nineties and the best, especially in London, were able to attract graduate scientists to their staffs. They openly admitted that they were aiming for the same sort of relationship with the growing number of new universities that the grammar schools had with the older universities. In 1897 they contained double the number of pupils from elementary schools and five times as many children of manual workers as the grammar schools did.[1] These schools were clearly a threat to one of the established types of secondary schools, namely the grammar school.

The term 'secondary education' had passed into common usage by the last quarter of the century. In spite of the development of the Higher Grade Schools and the Organized Science Schools this sphere of education was still not considered to be on the state's agenda. However, as a result of the Taunton Commission, the Charity Commission had been empowered to re-allocate endowments so that these resources were used more efficiently in the purpose for which the original benefactors had intended them. In the twenty-five years up to 1894 the Commission dealt with endowments whose income amounted to about five-sevenths of those that were thought to be subject to the Endowed Schools Act. There was some attempt to observe

[1] V. G. Couch, *A sociological interpretation of the development of technological education in England, France and Germany in the twentieth century,* unpublished Ph.D. thesis, University of London, 1955, pp. 398–9.

the policy of three grades of schools as recommended by the Taunton Commission. Attention was also given to the foundation of girls' grammar schools. Yet this was a very slow and cumbersome way to found a secondary system. A legal method was being applied to what was basically a political problem.

The Charity Commission also influenced the growth of those leading grammar schools which were now generally regarded as 'the public schools'. In point of fact this was often welcome since new constitutions could be established enabling the appointment of national figures as governors. Fees could be regulated and new subjects introduced. Frequently, as had been the case at such schools as Rugby, houses were established and games fields laid out. During the period from 1860 to 1880 games became compulsory, organized and eulogized at leading public schools. In some schools the curriculum was changed to meet the demands of parents who had begun to appreciate the need for scientific subjects.

These schools had a strong desire to preserve their freedom from state intervention. This common policy brought an increasing number into the body founded by Thring in 1869, the Headmasters' Conference (H.M.C.). Largely through this they became conscious that they faced many of the same problems. By 1903 102 schools, containing about 30,000 pupils, were members of the H.M.C. They were united in two aims, namely the desire to remain free of external control and to dissociate themselves from any attempt by the government to class them with the grammar schools. These two types of school might both be secondary, but the H.M.C. schools did not see themselves as being in the same system.

As literacy spread, technical instruction became more possible. Until 1899 when the Board of Education was established the main source of state provision in this field below degree level was the Department of Science and Art. The driving force behind its expansion was Major-General J. D. F. Donnelly. This Department was in existence for forty-six years and Donnelly worked in it for forty years. He entered it as a young engineer officer in 1853 and the fact that he and other engineer officers were employed in various capacities, for example as examiners, in the first half of the Department's life shows very clearly how scarce were men capable of controlling the teaching of science at this time. Donnelly had applied the method of payment by results to science teaching prior to the Revised Code of 1862, and the numbers of candidates sitting the various examinations which began in 1859 rose from 5,466 in 1865 to 202,868 in 1895.[1] Initially there had been six subjects, but by gradual additions there were twenty-five by 1895. Subjects included mathematics, chemistry, physics and also such practical subjects as metallurgy and navigation, but all the latter subjects were taught according to the ruling definition of technical instruction, namely in a theoretical fashion so that emphasis was given to the principles underlying practice rather than to the more practical aspects of industrial application. Until 1867 there was a special examination to certify science teachers in order to increase the supply of such teachers. After this date other measures were taken by the Department to meet the same end. For example, holiday courses for practising teachers were organized in provincial centres.

The biggest rate of increase in numbers earning grants from the Department of Science and Art occurred in the mid- and late eighties and was largely due to the rise of science teaching in post-elementary schools. This was the period when the Organized Science Schools and Higher Grade Schools increased very rapidly. Many grammar schools, particularly in the industrial areas, also received financial assistance from this source. In point of fact this Department was the one educational department that aided both elementary and secondary education throughout the whole of Great Britain and even gave grants in the colonies. This result was achieved without any religious difficulties. The growth of the Department led to a great rise in expenditure for a form of education that was considered by many to be very arid. Perhaps the extreme example of this was the way in which many students in urban areas underwent courses in agriculture without any practical experience at all; the main aim of this type of course was to earn a grant through success in the examinations.

[1] For statistics see yearly Reports of the Department of Science and Art.

Very few artisans at first seem to have profited from the Department's efforts since the standard of education demanded was too high, but then came the 1870 Act, which started to lower the rate of illiteracy. In the early 1870s the rapid expansion in the expenditure of the Department was causing worry at the Treasury. If technical instruction for artisans was to grow, another source of finance had to be found. From 1870 the Devonshire Commission was considering technical instruction and it brought some attention to the problem of the instruction of artisans. Publicity from Huxley amongst others focused attention on the fact that the Guilds of the City of London had vast wealth that could be turned to this purpose. *The Economist*, an extremely strong supporter of *laissez-faire*, noted that, if the state could interfere in such endowments as the universities and endowed schools, it could prevail upon the Guilds to use their endowments to the more socially useful purpose of technical instruction. Agitation continued throughout the decade, until in 1880 the City and Guilds of London Institute was incorporated with the aim of establishing two colleges in London for higher technical education and also of taking over certain industrial examinations that the Royal Society of Arts had established in 1873. This was the start of the City and Guilds examinations which still play a very important part in technical education.

Once again the provision that had come to be seen as necessary came from non-government sources, albeit after some political pressure. Though links with the state were present from the start and much of the instruction took place in elementary schools during the evenings, once again a dual system had been established. This time the partners were the state and representatives of the economy. Furthermore the main connection was to the Department of Science and Art, a sector of education that seemed to show much autonomy and to work independently of the goals of the system as a whole. Undoubtedly this tendency was aided by the low visibility of much of what was done. The Education Department was at Whitehall and the Department of Science and Art at South Kensington. Contact seems to have been rare. Donnelly could deviate relatively easily from the Committee of Privy Council's policies, and from the point of view of the economy his action was probably more helpful than harmful.

The major change in higher education in the last quarter of the century was the establishment of several new university colleges. These were sited in industrial cities. Thus colleges at Newcastle (1871), Leeds (1874), Bristol (1876), Sheffield (1879), Birmingham (1880), Nottingham (1881) and Liverpool (1882) were founded in this period. Endowments and gifts from wealthy local businessmen were common, and these civic universities tended to look to their local areas for support. Oxford and Cambridge continued to recruit on a national basis. London University was already coming to see itself as providing for the Empire since it was situated in the capital city. London, it was considered, must cater for the Empire and such institutions as the Royal School of Mines (later to become Imperial College) were very conscious of this policy. Civic universities were in regional capitals and partly because the source of their finance was local, but also because they saw regional needs, these universities came to provide for the industrial specialities of their regions – Birmingham in general metallurgy, Sheffield in iron and steel, Leeds in textiles, and Newcastle in engineering.

Slowly industrialists began to see that the new universities could provide the skilled managerial labour that they now needed, because of the greater stress on science in industrial processes. The universities were changing their function. Higher education had been seen almost entirely for some centuries as having the individual function that may be roughly expressed in the words 'making a better man'. Now there was a growing realization that the universities had a specifically social function inasmuch as they supplied the labour force with trained manpower. London had been a forerunner in this respect since from its beginning it had set out to train for the professions of medicine and law. London extended this social function to the newer professions of engineering and to some extent to teaching. The civic universities carried the process a stage further to industrial managers, an occupational group which had not been connected at all with institutions of university level in this country, though things were very different in France and Germany.

Change was slower in Oxford and Cambridge. Here control was still very much in academic hands, and in teaching stress was put on the tutorial rather than on the lecture, which had come to be more important at the new universities. Residence made such a teaching system easy to run and was itself the more necessary since recruitment was not local but national. During the period from 1850 to 1899 more than four-fifths of students at the two ancient universities came from the public schools and this proportion was greater than in the period before; only 7 per cent came from local grammar schools.[1]

There was little pressure from these students for high academic standards or for a curriculum of economic significance. This was a time of growing athleticism at Oxford and Cambridge. For some these universities served a political function in that useful experience was gained in political debating clubs. There were, however, some changes of importance. New laboratories were opened, the Cavendish at Cambridge in 1870 and the Clarendon at Oxford in 1872. Engineering had come to be accepted as a subject at Cambridge by the 1890s. In general, laboratories at universities as in schools caused difficulties because they were so expensive to establish and to run. One other change during these years was the admittance of women to the ancient universities. Girton College moved to Cambridge in 1873 from Hitchin, where it had been founded three years earlier, and in 1879 Somerville and Lady Margaret Hall were started at Oxford as colleges for women.

Another innovation at Cambridge was the founding of the Cambridge Teacher Training Syndicate in 1879. The H.M.C. had pressed the two older universities to do something about the training of schoolmasters in 1871, and four years later a conference was held at the house of Kay-Shuttleworth, by now an old man, though still much concerned with educational matters. In 1876 the H.M.C. sent a memorandum to Oxford and Cambridge; Cambridge responded rapidly. Efforts were also being made to train the secondary schoolmistresses now needed to staff the new girls' grammar schools that were being established

[1] H. Jenkins and D. Caradog Jones, 'Social Class of Cambridge Alumni', *British Journal of Sociology*, June 1950.

as a result of the Charity Commission's reallocation of endowments. In 1885 arrangements were made at Cambridge for a hall of residence for intending women secondary teachers. It should be noted that the decision was taken at this time that grammar school masters and mistresses should be trained apart from elementary school teachers; the training college was deemed unsuitable for the training of secondary teachers.

During the 1890s another competitor to the training college came into being and again the universities were involved, though in this case it was London and the new universities. For a time there had been pressure from some of the larger School Boards to be allowed to set up non-residential colleges to relieve the shortage of teachers. Central classes for pupil-teachers became common in London during the eighties. By the Code of 1890 the establishment of Day Training Centres was permitted and at some of the centres it was possible for students to take degrees. Sixteen centres were opened by 1900 with 1,355 students, of whom rather more than half were women. This development was important in that often university teachers could act as staff, a great help when highly qualified lecturers were scarce. Furthermore, the 'seminary' idea of training was challenged at a time when there was a growing realization that the training colleges were rather narrow and limiting in their effect. Any link with the universities lifted the status of education and at least opened the chance of the development of the more theoretical and philosophical approach to the subject without which the practice of teaching rested on poor foundations.

The pupil-teacher system was much improved by this type of change. The attainments of the intending teacher who became an 'apprentice' in an elementary school were not great. In the mid-seventies it had been said of the average candidate for training college that he 'can work the ordinary rules of Arithmetic, but not problems involving rules; he can write out a proposition of Euclid by memory, but cannot employ it intelligently; he knows just enough Algebra to be confused; he can parse an English sentence fairly, and he has a very fair knowledge of the bare facts of geography and history; he has a slight smattering of a French or Latin vocabulary; he knows the ordinary forms of schoolkeeping'.[1] Undoubtedly, despite these apparently low standards, the needs of the time were met and the success of the pupil-teacher system must have contributed to the delay in establishing a full secondary system. The improvements that came by setting up first central classes and then Pupil Teacher Centres went some way to meeting the higher standards of the later years of the nineteenth century, though these developments continued to undermine the chances of organizing the secondary schools. To some it was clear that the education given in these centres met the demands of the labour force; one parent said that they were the best institutions he knew for preparing for the Civil Service.[2]

In 1900 there were forty-three training colleges in England and Wales, all except two of which were run by religious denominations and thirty of which were under the Church of England. Many former pupil-teachers came to the colleges with the view that they knew all about teaching, and once there the colleges did little to disabuse them of their formal and conventional idea of how to run a school. Towards the end of the century the curriculum became a little broader; by the Code of 1890 a third year was permitted, though few took it except for linguists who after 1893 could go abroad. The academic work still tended to be rather theoretical and much stress was put on examinations, as many as six per year and often run by H.M.I.s. After 1890 there was an attempt to make colleges more practical by giving more stress to work in the model schools, often attached to the colleges. However, many of these schools were of a low standard. By 1900 about 30 per cent of elementary teachers were trained and certificated, about 25 per cent were certificated but untrained, and about 45 per cent were former pupil-teachers who were neither trained at colleges nor certificated by any of the other procedures that existed. The proportion of certificated teachers varied according to area with the lowest proportions in

[1] *Committee of Council Report*, 1876–7, pp. 685–6, quoted R. Rich, *The Training of Teachers during the Nineteenth Century*, London, 1933, pp. 211–12.

[2] *Royal Commission on the working of the Elementary Education Act*, 1886–8, Vol. I, p. 482.

the country and the highest in the towns. It can therefore be seen that not only, as has been indicated, was there a shortfall in the supply of teachers but there were also grounds for serious doubt about the quality of the teaching profession at the elementary level.

By the last decade of the century many were coming to see that there was a real need to coordinate educational provision. The 1870 Act had allowed the state to intervene through the School Boards and forced the denominations to redouble their efforts. Illiteracy had almost disappeared. However, the elementary system was probing forward in an uncontrolled way into the secondary sphere. The Department of Science and Art had been able to provide more technical instruction because of the success of the elementary system, and it had also redefined its own function by establishing Organized Science Schools of a secondary nature. These post-elementary schools were in no real way linked to the recognized secondary schools whose expansion relied mainly on parents buying education, but also on endowments reorganized with the help of the Charity Commission. The public schools stood well apart, very independent and keen to avoid any state interference under the leadership of a well-organized pressure group, the Headmasters' Conference. At the level of higher education, Oxford and Cambridge had some links with these schools through the newly established examinations and the training of a few masters and mistresses, but it was the new civic universities that were coming to have some manifest social function, particularly in the way in which they served the needs of the local managerial labour force. The time was near when redefinition would be essential. What were the main strains at work?

2 Strains

The last quarter of the nineteenth century has been given the controversial title of 'The Great Depression'. British industry was under severe competition from overseas, especially from the U.S.A. and Germany, both of which were industrializing rapidly at this time. They were, therefore, in large measure bound to have a more efficient industrial base than Britain, if only because their machinery was more up-to-date. Some of the impact of this competition was cushioned for Britain by the returns that she was now gathering from her earlier heavy colonial investment. However, there were big changes in the nature of the labour force and these were the outward sign of the forces of world competition. The traditional professions of the law, the church and medicine grew more slowly than new professions, such as engineering and accountancy. At another level there was the emergence of the technician, as for example, the chemist in the laboratory of a steel mill or a dye works. There was also a continuing increase in the demand for clerks that can be traced to the greater complexities of both industrial and governmental management. The growing demands on local and central government, as typified by the establishment of the School Boards in 1870 or the County Councils in 1888, were such that inevitably more clerical labour was needed. At the lower levels of the labour force the numbers of children employed had much diminished, but there was still a considerable demand for 'half-timers', children who spent half the day at work and half at school; owing to certain loopholes in the Education Acts this system was still possible. These escape clauses were part of the truce situation of the time and were included to meet the demands of two important groups, the Lancashire cotton millowners and the farmers, especially in East Anglia. In 1876 there were 201,284 half-timers and even by 1897 there were still 110,654, of whom more than half were in Lancashire.[1]

The attitude held towards knowledge was changing. The traditional view was that knowledge was transmitted by practice, often from father to son and in a face-to-face situation. Such knowledge was achieved by effort and tested by experience. A newer attitude was becoming more common by the end of the century. Knowledge could be transmitted impersonally through books and teaching and it was testable apart from experience, for instance by examinations. This change from a traditional to an instrumental view of knowledge allowed a change in attitudes towards elementary education for workers but was, perhaps, more visible at managerial level, resulting in the birth of the

[1] G. Balfour, op. cit., p. 49.

view that technical instruction and even university education was not necessarily a luxury for the upper levels of the labour force. To some extent the economic forces at work were forcing the establishment of different educational avenues into the labour force.

The growing feeling that the educational system was not meeting the needs of the economy was expressed in a series of reports, namely those of the Samuelson Select Committee on Scientific Instruction of 1867–8 and the Devonshire and Samuelson Royal Commissions on Technical Instruction of 1870–5 and 1881–4. This last Commission is a classical example of the contemporary *laissez-faire* attitude. The government appointed it on the understanding that its members, all avowed supporters of the cause of technical instruction, should pay their own expenses. Its report was a magnificent document which was read abroad as well as at home and played a large part in forcing the subsequent redefinition of technical instruction by the Act of 1889. In some ways it was unfortunate that this Act preceded that of 1902 which led to the creation of the state secondary system, since, as the Report made clear, Germany's success in catching Britain up industrially was largely attributable to her fine secondary schools, a growth not paralleled in Britain. Matthew Arnold's cry of the sixties 'Organize your secondary schools' was at last heard and in 1894 the Bryce Commission was appointed to investigate secondary education.

Besides these economic strains there were other reasons for questioning the definitions of education laid down in the years leading up to 1870. Major changes had occurred in the balance of political power as a result of the Reform Acts of 1867 and 1884. The former act gave the vote to half the urban working class and the latter to many workers in rural areas, so that after 1884 this country had universal male suffrage. As the franchise was extended, the working class initiated organized political action on its own behalf. The first workers to be elected as Members of Parliament formed a small pressure group within the Liberal Party, but the working class could exert more power through organized activity by the trade unions. In 1868 the Trades Union Congress met for the first time and as early as the year 1885

passed a motion demanding a 'truly national system of education'. The Independent Labour Party was founded in 1893 with
a more left-wing platform. Support for socialist policies also
came from the middle class, particularly from such intellectuals
as Bernard Shaw, and Sidney and Beatrice Webb; in 1884 the
Fabian Society was founded by the latter group to push slowly
towards socialism. Pressures from such sources played a part in
the passing of the 1890 Education Act by which School Boards
were given the power to admit children without fees.

State intervention was now considered more permissible, particularly at a time when the facts of poverty were more publicly
known. Charles Booth published his immense *Life and Labour of
the People of London* during the years 1891 to 1903. The results
of the patient research of this wealthy philanthropist showed
that about a quarter of the population of London were living in
poverty. The question that was now commonly being asked ran
something like this. 'Is it possible with empty stomachs to pay
attention to the multiplication table?'[1] Furthermore, the possibility of practical answers to this type of question seemed nearer
to the working class since they now had elected representatives
as members of the School Boards, especially in the large cities.
In these circumstances of growing political power, particularly
at the level of local government, it was not surprising that a
motion demanding freer entry to the secondary schools was
passed by the Trades Union Congress in 1897. A growing power
in the land was opposed to the élitist policy recommended by the
Taunton Commission of the 1860s.

The various social classes, therefore, were coming to define
education in rather different terms from those of the 1860s and
1870s. The principle of public provision of education had been
accepted; the whole nation had a right to be educated. Yet each
social class was to be educated in a different way. The middle
class saw their own education taking place in fee-paying
schools of various types. The upper middle class would send
their sons, and in some cases even their daughters, to boarding
schools. The lower middle class would support proprietary day

---

[1] *Justice*, 29 March 1884, quoted B. Simon, *Education and the Labour
Movement, 1870–1920*, London, 1965, p. 133.

schools, though more and more, particularly amongst those on the boundary of the middle and working classes, sent their children to the post-elementary schools whose relevance for a future career was obvious. The academic content of the curriculum taught in the public schools was still of secondary importance compared with the stress put upon character building. Manliness was more and more connected with athleticism; success at games was seen as a criterion for judging moral worth. Intellectual effort tended to be given relatively less stress. The more practical subjects that the Samuelson Commission had emphasized as having great social and economic relevance and as being vital in Germany's industrial growth were still not seen as a central part of the curriculum. There were exceptions in that some of the proprietary schools in large cities taught science and languages.

The middle class defined the education of the working class as a necessary free service in a minimal form. It is difficult to conjure up the full range of meaning implied by the word 'elementary' when applied to education during the last part of the nineteenth century. Briefly elementary education was seen as free – hence, tainted by charity it must be cheap – hence, also it must be given in large school classes and consist merely of the three R's. It must have a curriculum sufficient to ensure a meagre literacy and be suited solely to the lower classes – hence, in an élitist age, it must be entirely unconnected with the ruling class. From this final point stemmed much of the middle-class opposition to the successful and rapid growth of the post-elementary Higher Grade and Organized Science Schools, since their pupils were put in a position from which they could ascend the social ladder. And, to add insult to injury, this was done in schools which in the eyes of the middle class were subsidized out of taxation and rates, the greater part of which they themselves paid.

The working class had not yet come to criticize the fee-paying secondary schools and accepted them as the normal middle-class education. They still saw the elementary school as basic to the education of the majority of the working class, but now the idea of secondary education **had** begun to enter into their definition of the kind of education needed by the working class. In 1897 the Trade Union Congress had demanded secondary education for all, but its voice did not carry the day in forming left-wing policy at that time. The Fabians under the influence of Sidney Webb came out strongly in favour of the development of secondary education for the working class by the creation of a scholarship ladder leading from the elementary schools into the secondary schools.

The policy of the Fabians was that entry to secondary education for the working class should be achieved by a gradual widening of the opportunities of free entry to the grammar school. Beatrice Webb called this Sidney's 'capacity-catching machine'. As a result of his influence the London County Council Technical Education Board established a system of county scholarships and by 1901 ten scholars were at universities. The route by which these students had reached university was from the elementary school and then through the recognized secondary school system. By secondary schools the supporters of this policy meant élitist schools and not some version of the popular post-elementary schools which gave education of a secondary nature within the constraints of the Elementary Code. The curriculum of the former was classical in nature, of the latter modern and practical. The former had in the past ensured upward social mobility and therefore seemed the most likely to provide it in the future. On somewhat similar grounds there was opposition to practical subjects in the elementary schools since the three R's had led to upward social mobility for many clerks and teachers and hence, even at this level, a version of the literary curriculum gained most support.

Religion, as an institution, had become less important in England by 1900, but it was the position of the religious denominations that triggered off the first major questioning of the 1870 definition because to expand the church schools, or even to keep up to the standards set by the new School Boards, demanded a level of expenditure that could only be maintained with great difficulty. By the early 1880s between a quarter and a third of children were in Board schools but the average annual expenditure from rates on each child in these schools was just over 19*s.*, whereas voluntary contributions were on average 8*s.* 6½*d.* per child in denominational schools.[1] The difficulties that the denominations were meeting in financing their schools led to the appointment of the Cross Commission on the working of the Elementary Education Acts in 1886, which reported two years later. The members agreed on purely educational matters, but a substantial minority report, signed by eight of the twenty-three members, recommended popularly managed non-denominational schools whereas the majority wanted more financial aid for the voluntary schools. It can be seen that the dual system was here under substantial minority criticism.

During the 1890s both parties to the dual system extended their efforts. Between 1890 and 1900 the number of children in voluntary schools rose from 2·3 to 2·5 millions but those in Board schools increased more rapidly from 1·5 to 2·2 millions. Despite, or perhaps because of, their great effort the denominations were now finding that they were unable to maintain some of their schools, and, particularly in the case of the Church of England, they were sometimes forced to hand schools over to the School Boards. During this decade the denominational schools started to move into debt. Up to about 1885 finance, though difficult to find, had been adequate, but by 1900 it has been estimated that these schools were £450,000 in debt. The main danger to voluntary schools was in the towns; support was firmer in rural areas where the Church of England had a large number of schools.

Another difficulty was that teachers had become more difficult to attract to voluntary schools. Salaries were not yet uniform throughout the profession, and the Boards could pay higher rates. Furthermore, very often voluntary schools insisted on additional duties that teachers had to perform as a condition of appointment; examples were playing the organ at Sunday services or acting as secretary to church committees. The ironic result was that, though the training colleges that were mainly supported by the denominations were the only source of fully trained teachers, many of their products went not into the voluntary, but into the Board schools.

[1] M. Cruickshank, op. cit., pp. 55–7.

In 1890 the Act that eliminated school fees further complicated the financial position of the denominations as this measure removed one of their sure sources of finance. This occurred at a time when Acland, then Vice-President of Council, had introduced regulations insisting on higher standards of building and sanitation. However, some relief was given by legislation which gave the denominations 'fee-grant'. This could only be considered a temporary redefinition because so much else had to be decided in the educational field by this date. In addition there was a feeling that the Exchequer grant on education must not be allowed to go on rising at a time when the Boer War was becoming costly. Clearly, the dual system as devised in 1870 was due for revision. All the old religious difficulties were present, not so much because religion was still a central institution but because the denominations had risen to the challenge presented by the 1870 Act so successfully that any future redefinition would once again have to take account of the religious denominations.

There were also changes in the family that had implications for education. Perhaps the most important was the rising status of women as the movement for emancipation grew stronger. Education for girls became more important, especially amongst the middle class, though for the working class the rising demand for women teachers due to the expansion of education meant more chances of upward social mobility through the pupil-teacher system. Amongst the middle class the family was almost ceasing to be considered an educative agency in a formal sense. Boys went to boarding school as did most of their sisters, though infants were still often educated by governesses at home.

From the 1870s a purely demographic trend was of some importance. The birth-rate declined, first among the middle class; but later among the working class. To some extent the higher costs of the education now essential to maintain middle-class status tended to act as a restriction on family size. The working class also found that children could no longer become wage earners at an early age. This change in the birth-rate was a complex phenomenon, and it followed (though this does not imply causation) a number of measures to improve child welfare. Thus in 1889 the National Society for the Prevention of Cruelty to Children was founded. In the same year Mundella sponsored an act, often called 'The Children's Charter', by which children were given legal protection against negligent parents. Clearly parents were no longer considered to have absolute control over the education and welfare of their children. Other agents of informal education were developing at this time. The Young Men's Christian Association which had been established in the 1840s began to be influential in the eighties, and the Young Women's Christian Association was founded in 1877. During this same period boys' papers, such as the *Boys' Own Paper*, began to have an impact on middle-class schoolboys. Education had once been mainly a family matter. Now it was not just the concern of schools, but of such informal agencies as clubs and magazines.

The declining educative function of the family and the growth of the educational system so as to include all children spelt the start of the age of mass education. Matthew Arnold had seen this and warned of the dangers that he thought were implicit in such a development. More particularly he considered that standards might be lowered. Certainly during the period from 1870 onwards more thought was given to education as an academic subject. The first university chairs in education were established in Edinburgh and St Andrews Universities in 1876. In England the growing concern of the universities, seen in the development of the day training centres, led to a more rigorous consideration of educational theory and practice. In the late 1890s Professor J. J. Findlay of Manchester introduced Dewey's ideas to this country from America. In fact in 1892, two years before Dewey started his school in Chicago, F. W. Sanderson introduced some startlingly modern methods into his curriculum at Oundle. He established engineering laboratories, workshops, and cooperative projects at this public school. The possibility of education being considered as a subject in its own right, as had been the case in, for instance, Germany for almost a century, was clearly coming nearer.

One criterion for differentiating between a professional association and a trade union is whether the group in question gives attention to professional matters in addition to such matters as rates of pay and conditions of work. During the period after 1870 the professional organizations of teachers were almost entirely absorbed with such union-like issues as pay and conditions so that concern with purely educational matters, though not entirely absent, was slight. Organizational activity had begun after the Revised Code, but it was the religious difficulties at the time of the 1870 Act that offered the chance to recruit teachers into a National Union of Elementary Teachers. As this body grew in strength, the word 'Elementary' was dropped from the title. In 1885 there were 11,000 members and by 1902 membership had exactly doubled.[1] Already, a member of the National Union of Teachers had been elected to parliament and could have some influence on debates on education by deploying knowledge of actual practice in the contemporary Board schools.

The largest part of the efforts of the National Union of Teachers was, however, given to the twin aims of raising the status of teaching as a profession and of bettering the pay and conditions of serving teachers. The relative rise in status is illustrated in the fact that in 1875 the average salary of a teacher was £109 per year, but by 1895 it had risen to £122. At the latter date a curate earned somewhere around £200 or less.[2] The main problem was that these averages masked large differences between town and country, and between Board and voluntary schools. The National Union of Teachers was working to bring the more lowly paid up to the standard of the more highly paid teachers.

One major problem was that the teaching profession was as split in its allegiance to different associations of teachers as it was divided fundamentally in its organization into elementary and secondary. Thus its professional organization was governed by the definition of 1870 that established separate systems for each social class. During the years following the establishment of the National Union of Teachers, associations of Headmasters (1890), Headmistresses (1874), Assistant Masters (1891) and Assistant

[1] W. H. G. Armytage, *Four Hundred Years of English Education*, Cambridge, 1964, p. 156.
[2] ibid., p. 157.

Mistresses (1884) were established for those in secondary schools. In addition, during the 1890s other associations were formed to deal with the teaching of such subjects as modern languages, mathematics, science and classics. These bodies led to a higher professional standard and to the spreading of better methods of teaching among teachers who were for the most part untrained.

There were many strains at work in the system. Though a much larger proportion of the national income was being directed into education to meet the goals implicit in the 1870 definition, the pattern of the system, as it had grown within the range of tolerance permitted to it, no longer met either the definition on which it was based or the contemporary redefinitions. Autonomous development because of economic needs had led the Department of Science and Art into the alien territory of secondary education, and for the same reason the Education Department also had probed forward into post-elementary education. Political activity had brought about a questioning of the extremely class-bound definition of secondary education, though there was as yet no criticism of the private secondary school system for those who could afford it. Demands of a political nature for free education had helped to make financially unstable the position of the denominations who provided about half of elementary schooling. These strains led to a reopening of the religious issues involved in the original establishment of the dual system. Redefinition within the aim of establishing a co-ordinated overall system was essential, and the growing power of organized teachers meant that they might have some influence on the truce situation that emerged.

3 Redefinition

Clearly by the 1890s there were many problems in the English educational system that needed clarifying. The questioning of the 1870 solution had begun with the appointment of the Cross Commission in 1886. Since its report contained such a strong minority faction, its recommendations could not be called a new definition of the elementary sector. However, the discussions of the 1890s and the eventual solution in the Acts of 1899 and 1902 were much influenced by the settlement of technical education that was made in 1889.

After the report of the Samuelson Commission on Technical Instruction in 1884 there was a general acceptance that some legislative action must be taken so that technical education could be provided out of the rates. The efforts by the state through the Department of Science and Art and by private sources through the City and Guilds were insufficient; the government had to make additional provision. The question remained what was the machinery to be. Were the School Boards or some other body to be the authority? The machinery of government was radically reorganized in 1888 when County Councils and County Borough Councils were set up. It was to these new authorities that the responsibility for provision of rate-aided technical education was handed by the Technical Instruction Act of 1889. This new answer to the administrative problem of who was to provide technical education was to be of immense importance when the whole machinery of state provision came to be overhauled in 1902.

There was no immediate rush by the County Councils to use the powers given them. In 1890, however, seed money for technical education came from another source. In the budget a sum had been set aside to compensate the licensees of redundant public houses. Since this money could not be used for its original purpose due to opposition from both the liquor trade and the temperance movement, Goschen, the Chancellor, arranged that it could be used either for rate reduction or for technical education. Many authorities came to use this 'Whisky Money', as it was christened, for the latter purpose. County Technical Instruction Committees were appointed, on several of which sat men with knowledge of industrial needs. By 1892 thirty-nine counties had appointed full-time directors or secretaries of these committees to coordinate the expanding effort. The Act of 1889 had defined technical instruction in a much broader sense than was usual till this date. It was seen as 'instruction in the principles of science and art applicable to industries, and in the application of specific branches of science and art to specific industries and employment'. 'Manual instruction . . . in the use of

68

tools' was permitted. Such teaching had already been given out of charitable funds in London and was now in more popular demand, but it had not been provided by the state or officially considered as technical instruction. After 1890 there was a great rise in the amount spent on technical education. In 1892–3 local authorities assigned £472,560 of whisky money to this purpose and spent £12,762 from rates; by 1900–1 £863,847 came from whisky money and £106,209 from rates.[1] Thus, by the 1890s the curriculum of technical education had been defined, but the organization was still uncoordinated, since the Department of Science and Art, the City and Guilds, and the County Councils were all involved, and since the state provision was drawing on various financial sources including the 'Whisky Money'.

In the early 1890s the lack of adequate secondary facilities had become apparent, as had the fact that what provision existed was ill-coordinated. The Charity Commission, the Department of Science and Art, the Education Department through the Higher Grade Schools, and even the Board of Agriculture through a few agricultural schools were all involved. Since 1891 County Councils had also been able to provide assistance to secondary schools. In 1894 a Royal Commission on Secondary Education was appointed. The Bryce Commission reported very quickly in 1895, and one of its main recommendations was that some central body must be set up to coordinate the educational system and enable it to meet the many demands now put upon it, particularly by the economy. The problem was more complex than has so far been indicated. There were just over 2,500 School Boards with whom the Education Department had to deal individually. In 1890 about a quarter were in districts with a population of less than five hundred and a half in districts of less than a thousand. This resulted in much administration of a trivial nature at the centre which only aggravated the already existing problem of coordinating elementary education and the other branches of the system.

Immediately after the Bryce Report, Gorst, then Vice-President, drew up legislation to redefine the system. However, the religious problem stood in the way of a quick solution, and

[1] P. H. J. H. Gosden, op. cit., p. 162.

this Bill had to be dropped. Political issues were also involved, since Gorst wished to curb the School Boards. These bodies had much support, particularly from the Liberals, who dominated some of the larger Boards and to some extent saw them as admirable instruments of local democracy. Some immediate action had to be taken to relieve the financial burden on the denominations, and in 1897 the Voluntary Schools Act was passed to provide 5*s*. per pupil through newly established Voluntary Aid Associations, a further addition to the already complex administration of education. Meanwhile certain purely administrative, as opposed to legislative, changes were made in the regulations of the Department of Science and Art, by which County authorities could, if they wished, become responsible for all the higher education in their areas; sixty-three did in fact do so. This move was an attack on the power of the School Boards and could be seen as an attempt to define County authorities rather than School Boards as authorities for secondary education.

In 1899 the first phase of the major redefinition of education occurred. The Board of Education was established by Act of Parliament with the aim of coordinating the system under one minister, namely the President of the Board of Education. It was not till 1908 that the various sections of the Board could be brought together under one roof in a new building, and this made coordination in the early days somewhat difficult. Further purely administrative actions followed. Thus in 1900 a minute on the Higher Grade Schools was issued by the Board to prevent expansion of this type of school. This was mostly the work of Robert Morant, a senior civil servant in the Board at this time.

Morant is a key figure in the educational history of the period. He was an ambitious and able man who, after taking a classics degree at Oxford and a period of tutoring in Siam, had in 1895 become a member of the newly established Special Inquiries and Reports (or research) Branch of the Education Department. He rose rapidly and by 1900 had become a powerful figure in the new Board of Education. The exact details of what happened over the next two years are still unclear, but Morant played a large part and emerged after 1902 as the chief civil servant in the Board.

In one of his Special Reports Morant had drawn attention to the fact that an auditor had disallowed certain expenditure on post-elementary education made by a School Board as being outside the powers of such a body as defined by the 1870 Act. In fact, such disallowances by government auditors were a normal feature of the School Board scene due not to dishonesty but to ignorance or to political pressure to supply education that would not otherwise be provided. However, in 1899, whether instructed by Morant or purely by chance, an auditor of the Local Government Board named Cockerton declared a part of the expenditure of the greatest School Board in the land, the London Board, as being spent illegally on purposes not provided for by the Elementary Code. A major legal battle ensued which ended in the Court of Appeal when Mr Justice Wills upheld the lower court's verdict that this expenditure was illegal. It should be noted that he also indicated that in his view a very wide interpretation could be put on the word 'elementary', which would allow education up to sixteen or seventeen, in other words of a secondary nature, to be given on the elementary code. The government, however, stressed the illegality and concluded that a complete reorganization was necessary. This was no doubt true, but it also met Morant's views, since he believed that the future definition of education should be such that the new post-elementary education should give way to a version of the traditional secondary education.

From 1901 Morant became a more central figure in the political fight. Balfour, the Prime Minister, now also became deeply involved in the struggle to redefine education, since great feeling had been aroused throughout the country. Morant told Balfour that the problem must be solved by creating 'one symmetrical and consistent organization'. Eventually after immense difficulties within the Cabinet and Conservative Party a Bill was tabled. It aroused intense political and religious feeling both among supporters of the established church and among nonconformists of all denominations. The debates in parliament were long and impassioned.

The 1902 Education Act formed the second stage of the redefinition prompted by the Bryce Commission. It completed the administrative reorganization begun by the 1899 Act and also outlined the truce reached over the religious problem. The School Boards were abolished and, as might have been predicted from the administrative changes of the nineties, the County Councils and County Boroughs became the local education authorities (L.E.A.s) responsible for both elementary and secondary education. However, as a small *quid pro quo* to the supporters of the School Boards, Borough Councils where the population exceeded 10,000 and Urban Councils with more than 20,000 people were permitted to run elementary schools. Rate aid was to be given to the non-provided (denominational) schools. The capital costs and upkeep of such schools would continue to come from the denominations, but in return for rate aid the L.E.A.s were to control all secondary education in these schools, to appoint teachers except those for religious instruction and to have minority representation on the boards of managers. There was a conscience clause to guard the interests of those whose children attended a school run by a different denomination from their own.

The Bryce Commission had expressed the desire that the 'freedom, variety (and) elasticity' of the English system should be preserved.[1] There were, therefore, the minimum number of specific definitions in the Act. Thus the range of tolerance was wide and the various codes and handbooks that flowed from the new Board of Education under the administrative leadership of Morant set the direction of growth of the now more unified system without much difficulty. The Elementary Code of 1904 saw the purpose of this branch of education as 'to form and strengthen the character and to develop the intelligence of the children entrusted to it', a much wider definition than that of the Newcastle Commission. The Regulations for Secondary Schools, also issued in 1904, spoke of a 'general' and 'complete' education 'up to and beyond the age of sixteen'. Furthermore, the tolerance allowed was such that the 1902 Act led to an increased differentiation of the state educational system, as it authorized L.E.A.s to establish colleges for teachers. By 1913 twenty such colleges had been founded.

[1] *Royal Commission on Secondary Education*, 1895 Vol. I .p. 326.

One of the most remarkable clauses of the 1899 Act set up a Consultative Committee for England and Wales. On this committee sat eminent educationalists and others with an interest in educational affairs. The Board remitted matters of contemporary interest to them for consideration. In a sense this committee continued the creative part played by the former Code Committee made up of H.M.I.s. A tension founded on constructive criticism was built into the system and this was to result in a number of important and influential reports in the years to follow. Royal Commissions on educational topics became unnecessary as the Consultative Committee formed a permanent investigating body.

The Bryce Report had re-examined the seven counties that the Taunton Commission had investigated in the 1860s. The supply and condition of the grammar schools were found to have improved as a result of the educational work of the Charity Commission, but total provision was still inadequate. There were 2·5 places per 1,000 population in the counties surveyed, but the range of provision varied from 13·5 in Bedfordshire to 1·1 per 1,000 in Lancashire. The Bryce Commission had taken a very broad and at the time unfashionable view of secondary education, since they considered that 'no definition of technical instruction is possible that does not bring it under the head of Secondary Education, nor can Secondary Education be so defined as absolutely to exclude from it the idea of technical instruction'.[1] This view ran counter to that of the universities and public schools at which most of those in power had been educated.

A very strong supporter of the less traditional view of secondary education was Michael Sadler, who had been a member of the Bryce Commission. He subsequently became head of the Office for Special Inquiries and Reports at the Board of Education. A major struggle soon developed between Sadler and Morant. Sadler eventually left the Board and had an outstanding career in several universities. In addition, in the period prior to the 1914–18 war he advised several of the larger L.E.A.s on the development of their secondary schools. Certainly Morant was

[1] ibid., p. 136.

opposed to Sadler's broad view and had a great influence in drafting regulations that governed the development of the new L.E.A. secondary schools. The assumption was that such schools would grow in the image of the public schools and the two an-cient universities. These institutions were assumed to require and, indeed, expected little intervention. Therefore the new secondary schools were to be given a similar position of freedom and tolerance. The very titles used in the ruling definition of the time are indicative of how development was to proceed. Heads of schools under the Secondary Regulations were called 'Head-masters' unlike those of schools on the Elementary Code who were known as 'Head Teachers', and 'Headmasters' were left far freer of outside control than were 'Head Teachers'.

This lack of definition of secondary education reflected the assumptions of those in power about the new system that they were creating. During the fifty-seven days of debate on the 1902 Act only four days were given to the development of secondary education. The definitions that evolved were of a residual nature, for example, 'a course of wider scope and more advanced degree than that given in Elementary Schools'. This width of definition allowed the ruling concept that secondary education was for an élite to be influential on the way that the new L.E.A. grammar schools developed. The Elementary Code governed the education of the working class and was on the whole still mini-mal, cheap and tainted with charity. The Secondary Regulations guided the schools for the middle class and were much more con-cerned with sweetness and light. The Taunton Commission had suggested a three-tier system of secondary schools. In some ways the 1902 Act brought such a system into being. There were the fee-paying and boarding public schools from which the future rulers and members of the great professions went forth at eighteen. There were the new L.E.A. day grammar schools, again largely fee-paying, at which the industrial and commercial managers and the members of the rapidly expanding minor pro-fessions attended till sixteen. Finally, there were the free elementary schools to which the mass of the working class went up to the age of fourteen.

The teachers in the new grammar schools were on the whole

untrained like those in the public schools and in the endowed grammar schools. Many of these teachers still came from the ancient universities where little change occurred in the last years of the nineteenth century. More teachers, a very few of them trained, were coming from the new civic universities which in 1889 received the first grant, a sum of £15,000, from the government. A small committee was established to distribute such grants. But the universities were hardly seen as being part of the educational system and were still outside any administrative definition of education. The first suggestion to include the universities in some way in the administrative definition of education was made in 1904, when a committee of which Lord Haldane was chairman recommended the establishment of something like the present University Grants Committees namely a body to be responsible for the distribution of state monies to the universities that would report not to the Treasury but direct to parliament; in this way it was hoped that despite financial dependence academic freedom would be preserved.

4 Conclusion

The 1902 Act represented a new truce situation to meet a changed power situation. The conflict was not over basic value, and was therefore not disruptive. There were, however, large enough differences over goals and, in addition, there were many strains due to the changing position of the main institutions that interlocked with education. Especially noticeable was the new importance of the economy in respect of education. During the nineties the point was reached beyond which any further development must lead to a new definition of education, and three main problems for decision emerged. These were: how to coordinate the various growths that had occurred as a result of the definitions of thirty years before; secondly, what to do about the dual system now that the denominations were firmly entrenched as a result of the 1870 Act; and, finally, how to provide secondary education.

A measure of coordination was achieved by the Act of 1899 which established the Board of Education. The new religious compromise was achieved only after great political turmoil by the Act of 1902, which signalled the move from a system administered predominantly by the denominations to one mainly run by the state. The development of a secondary system was also ensured by the 1902 Act though the range of tolerance in the definition was such that the way in which the secondary schools grew was very much in the hands of those in administrative power. Parliament might feel that it controlled expenditure on the schools, because there were H.M.I.s to check that L.E.A.s spent government grants according to the Regulations and Codes. However, these instruments of control were drawn up within the Board of Education with little outside surveillance and were inspected by H.M.I.s who represented the Board. Some autonomous development was therefore possible providing expenditure did not increase too rapidly. Furthermore, civil servants, H.M.I.s and parliament to some extent shared much the same assumptions about what the direction of development of the new secondary schools should be and, therefore, the class nature of contemporary England was built into the unified educational system that had been created by the redefinition at the turn of the century.

CHAPTER FOUR

THE EXPANSION OF THE SYSTEM

The definition of education which was made around the turn of the century allowed for the development of a coordinated system of education that would include the elementary, secondary and technical sectors. The state system could even push forward into higher education since teacher training was included within the scope of the 1902 Act. The civic universities were not seen as on the state's agenda though money was being given to them. Yet the definition of education was much broader than that of 1870. As the English educational system grew, it had become more complex and, since the range of tolerance permitted by the 1902 Act was wide, there was the possibility both of autonomous development within the system and of further differentiation into such sectors as those dealing with the health and welfare of children. These fields might be thought peripheral to education, but unless they were given some consideration there would not be full use of the resources allocated to the educational system, since sick and hungry children make poor pupils.

The 1899 Act built into the structure of the English educational system the Consultative Committee. There was, therefore, in the future the chance of an official redefinition of whichever part of the system the Committee was examining. But during the first years of the century there was enough to be done in developing the system as defined by the 1902 Act. In 1914 the first world war broke out and, as a result, the political power situation was greatly changed. The egalitarian tendencies foreshadowed by the growth of the unions and left-wing groups in the late nineteenth century came to have much influence over the redefinitions of education suggested by the influential reports of the Consultative Committee made between the end of the first world war in 1918 and the start of the second in 1939.

Despite the new political situation and the continuing strains between the economy and the educational system these suggestions were abortive in that the additional resources that they demanded were not diverted into the educational system. The rate of expansion of the educational system was slowed down in the inter-war period because of extremely difficult economic conditions. However, these reports of the Consultative Committee were to form the basis for the next redefinition, that of 1944, which was triggered off by the idealistic desire to reconstruct a better Britain once the second world war was over.

1 Growth

The Act of 1899 established the Board of Education under a President who was to be a member of the government and responsible to parliament. There was at last the possibility of a coordinated educational policy administered by a central organization. The important link between the Board and the schools was the Inspectorate. By 1910 there were ninety-two higher grade inspectors of whom eighty-one were graduates of Oxford or Cambridge and, of these, fifty had degrees in classics. The sources upon which the Board could draw for men of the required calibre were restricted, but the type of man recruited fitted well into the policy for which Morant has been mainly held responsible, namely to found a school system of a broad liberal nature that did not put much emphasis on the vocational element. After 1918 the nature of the civil servants in the Board changed. No longer were men recruited internally with a special knowledge of education, but they came from other ministries following a career pattern as they moved from one ministry to another. In purely educational matters this change gave even more power to the experts, namely the H.M.I.s.

Since the Board had a wide range of tolerance within which it could act, the Inspectorate could easily follow a new and more liberal policy. In addition to the Regulations for the various branches of education that replaced the old Code the Board issued a series of Handbooks, giving advice and suggestions on how to teach in the different types of schools. The spirit of these books is seen from a quotation out of the 1905 Handbook, 'the only uniformity of practice that the Board of Education desire to see in the teaching of the Public Elementary school is that each teacher should think for himself.' That a new spirit had entered educational administration was noticed by *The Economist* in 1909. 'Gradually all the old safeguards for efficiency and economy which were once on the Statute Book have been swept away and each year the Board of Education pays less regard to those which it has perfunctorily inserted in its voluminous codes [which are] . . . too technical, and no doubt are meant to be too technical, for discussion in the House of Commons.'[1] The Board under strong leadership could shelter behind an expertise that insulated the developing system from excessive external intervention, though naturally the rising costs of educational expansion led to criticism over the size of taxes at the national level and of rates at the local level.

New subjects were introduced or became more common than in the last part of the nineteenth century. Handwork and crafts were more often taught. Attempts were made to use teaching methods such that the child learnt through activity. These changes were particularly noticeable after 1918. There were also new developments in religious instruction. During the 1920s the local authorities took the initiative in making arrangements with the denominations in their various areas to work out agreed syllabuses of religious instruction. Probably the best known of these was the Cambridgeshire syllabus, agreed in 1924. This was imitated or adopted by several other authorities. Looking back, it is possible to criticize many of the details of teaching method at that time. Thus many of the textbooks were middle class in orientation and direction with pictures of suburbia, fathers who were obviously white-collar workers and children with big toys. But at least there were pictures and an attempt to make school

[1] *The Economist*, 24 January 1909, p. 161.

books more relevant to children's lives. The task of providing textbooks for the schools of a society that was approaching 100 per cent literacy was a new one, and the capitalist publishing industry upon which the state educational system relied had only begun to tackle the problem.

The liberal approach that marked Morant's policy in the early years of the Board encouraged a much wider view of the educational system's responsibility for the child than had been held previously. The beginnings of such a change can be seen in a Report on Children under Five in Elementary Schools issued in 1905. A new form of school was seen as necessary for children from 'poor homes' and with 'mothers who have to work'. To some extent the Boer War had led many to ask whether the country was doing as much as was necessary to guard the health and welfare of its future manpower. In 1901 Seebohm Rowntree found that by his criteria a quarter of the population of York was living in poverty. In 1904 an interdepartmental committee on physical deterioration recommended that provision should be made for underfed children and for their medical inspection. In 1906 the Provision of Meals Act initiated the Schools Meals Service. By 1939 around 10 per cent of school children had their midday meal at school either free or at a subsidized price. In 1907 by the Education (Administrative Provisions) Act parliament accepted the principle that school children should undergo medical inspection. A medical department was established within the Board of Education. Under the first Chief Medical Officer, Sir George Newman, a remarkable series of reports was published that had a great influence on the health of British children. Eventually special arrangements were made for physically and mentally handicapped children. In 1910 a further power was given to the L.E.A.s. By the Education (Choice of Employment) Act vocational guidance could be given to boys and girls under seventeen.

The 1902 Act had only been passed after much political opposition from the Liberals, mainly because they spoke for the nonconformists against the established Church of England. At the election of 1906, partly because of the unpopularity generated by their responsibility for this Act, the Conservatives were replaced in power by the Liberals, who during the campaign promised a new settlement of the educational problem. The new President of the Board, Mr A. Birrell, introduced a Bill in 1906 which would in some ways have anticipated the 1944 Act. Birrell's solution was that there were to be two sorts of denominational school, one of which would receive a larger subsidy and hence be under greater state control than the other. However, this Bill was defeated in the House of Lords and two subsequent Liberal Bills, those of McKenna and Runciman, both of which were introduced in 1908, also failed. Thus it was that the definition of 1902 remained in the main undisturbed till 1914.

During the war many came to feel that plans should be made to build a better society after the war. When Lloyd George became Prime Minister in 1916 he showed that he felt education to be central to this policy of reconstruction and for the first and, so far, the only time in British history an educationalist was appointed to be the minister responsible for education. In 1916 H. A. L. Fisher, a distinguished historian, was called from his post of Vice Chancellor of Sheffield University to become President of the Board of Education. In 1918 he introduced his Education Act. This did not disturb the religious settlement of 1902. Two important clauses enacted that education should become compulsory for all up to the age of fourteen; it is a remarkable fact that as late as 1922 there were still about 70,000 half-timers, mainly by this time in agriculture rather than in textiles. Secondly, a system of part-time continuation schools was to be established to which children not in full-time education should go initially until the age of sixteen, and eventually until eighteen.

The suggestion of part-time continuation schools had been made before the war and was much influenced by German practice. Fisher's policy was supported on educational and moral grounds by the various professional associations and by a proportion of employers. Several local authorities inaugurated continuation schemes soon after the war, but some held the view that this was only a transitory policy and that soon the school-leaving age would be raised, eventually to sixteen. For this reason some authorities did not push on with the establishing of continuation schools. Another deterrent was that by 1919 economic conditions had become very difficult, so that money was short for an educational policy still not considered by many businessmen to be essential. The partial failure of the part-time continuation clauses became nearly total because of the economy measures taken in 1922. These were the result of the report of the Geddes Committee which had been set up by the government to recommend ways of economizing to meet the slump. In the contemporary climate of opinion continuation schools could not escape the Geddes axe. Furthermore, Fisher's other aim, namely the raising of the school-leaving age to fifteen, also came to nothing, firstly because of the recurring slumps and eventually because of the outbreak of war in 1939.

The provision of post-elementary schooling in schools on the elementary code should have been stopped by the 1902 Act, since the L.E.A.s could now provide secondary education from the rates. Morant's intention was to develop a system of state-provided secondary grammar schools. The regulations drawn up after the Cockerton Judgment and as a result of the 1902 Act led to the conversion of the majority of the Higher Elementary Schools into L.E.A. grammar schools. Certainly during Morant's period as senior civil servant at the Board the intrusions of elementary schools into the secondary sphere were held in check. In 1910 Morant committed an unfortunate indiscretion. He passed for official publication some very critical remarks made by an H.M.I. about the capabilities of elementary teachers as inspectors. As a result Morant had to be moved from the Board. Lloyd George, who had been his opponent at the time of the 1902 Act, knew his worth and arranged for Morant to become Chairman of the new National Health Insurance Commission. In the first decade of this century Morant laid the administrative foundations of the modern educational system, and in the second decade prior to his early death in 1920 he built up the unemployment and pensions system. He thus has a sound claim to be the administrative father of the British welfare state.

With Morant's departure from the Board post-elementary schools began to grow again. After 1911 Central Schools became possible under the elementary code. These were schools to which older children in large towns could be sent for the latter part of their elementary schooling if they wanted to stay beyond the minimum legal leaving age. Such schools were established first in the north and in London. As had been the case in the late nineteenth century the industrial areas felt the need for more education than was supplied by the mainly fee-paying secondary schools. Central Schools became very common in the inter-war years and by the thirties were sending former pupils to universities.

In 1913 a new type of school emerged, the Junior Technical School. This was doubly against Morant's policy. Firstly, it provided post-elementary schooling outside the secondary schools and, secondly, the curriculum was not of the broad liberal nature favoured by Morant. The Regulations governing these schools lasted till 1934 and stated that they were 'for pupils from Elementary schools in preparation either for artisan or other industrial or for domestic employment'. The course was of three years duration and excluded any language other than English or Welsh. Therefore these schools could not compete with the sixth forms developing in the grammar schools. The curriculum catered for a broad occupational band, for instance, engineering or building. Despite their obviously lower status than the grammar school these schools became very popular in industrial areas since their pupils often became apprentices or even lower-level technicians, positions that seemed to promise security during the heavy unemployment of the inter-war years.

Secondary education was, however, the main beneficiary of the 1902 Act, since this Act permitted the L.E.A.s to spend from rates on secondary schools. In theory there was no reason why a system of secondary schools for all should not have emerged on the basis of the actual legislation passed in 1902, but this did not happen because the working of the Act was determined by the way in which those in power defined 'secondary'. Although they widened the scholarship ladder, they contrasted the secondary school with the elementary school; the former was for the middle class and the latter for the working class. Thus the new grammar schools were either existing endowed schools that were subsidized or former higher elementary schools that were upgraded or new creations that definitely imitated the endowed grammar schools; on the whole the influence of the Arnold tradition was profound. In 1904 there were 491 grammar schools with 85,358 pupils; by 1925 there were 1,616 such schools with 334,194 pupils. These new schools were for both boys and girls; some were co-educational, though most were single-sex schools.

In 1904 the Board issued Regulations to govern the standards and direction of growth of the new grammar schools. Again the exact part played by Morant is uncertain. The team of H.M.I.s who drafted these regulations were on the whole supporters of the policy that in the new secondary schools there should be taught a version of the liberal and mainly classical curriculum associated with the late nineteenth-century public schools. There was some support for a more mathematical and scientific content, but the idea found in the Bryce Report that technical education was one species of the genus 'secondary' was absolutely foreign to those in the Board who were responsible for the development of the new L.E.A. grammar schools. Thus it was that there grew the dichotomy between secondary and technical education symbolized by the creation of the low-status Junior Technical School in 1913.

After Morant's departure from the Board there was an attempt to introduce a vocational element into the curriculum of the new secondary schools. In 1913 a circular was issued to permit and encourage such developments, but this had little immediate effect because of the outbreak of war in 1914. There was an additional and powerful influence on the curriculum of the secondary school namely the examination system. The Consultative Committee considered this and issued a report in 1911 that called for coordination between the universities responsible for the various examinations. Negotiations took place in the early years of the war and in 1917 a standardized system, the School Certificate, was evolved. This first school examination, normally to be taken around the age of sixteen, served a dual purpose. It could be a terminal examination or it could serve as a university entrance matriculation qualification. Because of this latter need most pupils were taught a broad general curriculum that included Latin, English, a modern language, History, Geography, Mathematics and, for most boys, Science. Many employers came to realize that 'matric.', gained by passing five credits before the age of sixteen, represented a worthwhile standard of education and insisted that applicants for jobs had such a qualification. This examination, therefore, came to be a force for uniformity of curriculum in the grammar schools.

There were other influences at work on these schools. In the late nineteenth century the new girls' secondary schools had permitted the teaching of some of the traditional subjects of women's education. Thus art and music were taught and came to be found also in secondary schools for boys. Extracurricular activities became commoner. Undoubtedly the precedent here was the playing of games in the public schools, but there was at this time a broadening in the nature of such activities. Scout or Guide troops, various clubs, and for boys units of the Officers' Training Corps, were all founded in these schools. By such means a day school's control over its pupils was somewhat extended.

A circular was issued by the Board in 1913 suggesting that specialization in groups of allied subjects might form a basis for advanced work in the sixth forms of grammar schools, but little could be done because of the war. In 1917 Fisher allocated money to encourage this type of course. Grants could be given to advanced courses based on science and mathematics, classics or modern studies. In 1922 modern languages and geography were added. At the same time the Higher Certificate examination was introduced to test two years of such work beyond the School Certificate. The numbers of such sixth form courses rose rapidly from 127 in 1918 to 469 in 1925.[1] One result of the development of sixth forms was the emergence of a new criterion of the educational worth of a school, namely how many of its pupils went on to university.

The link between the public schools and the older universities was still very close, but the grammar schools had especially close connections with local civic universities. It is a tribute to the

[1] See the Board of Education Reports for 1921–2, 1923–4 and 1935.

prestige of the public schools that throughout the depressed economic conditions of the inter-war years the middle class continued to pay for the schooling of their children at the very time when the L.E.A. grammar schools were developing to provide a somewhat similar secondary education that could also lead to the universities. However, as the scholarship ladder was widened, there was an increasing proportion of working-class children in these schools and this may well have lowered their status in the eyes of the middle class.

The age of transfer from the elementary school to the L.E.A. secondary school slowly became accepted as just over eleven. The Bryce Report had reckoned that eleven or twelve was the right age, but the transfer examination took place at various ages throughout the country. Morant's first regulations envisaged a four-year secondary course from the age of twelve, but in 1907 new regulations enabled local authorities to transfer children at ten so as to lengthen the stay of ex-elementary pupils in the secondary schools. Gradually eleven plus became the commonest age of transfer; in 1910 26 per cent of children moved at this age, but by 1924 the proportion had risen to 54 per cent. In 1926 the Hadow Report of the Consultative Committee recommended that there should be a fixed age of transfer in order to coordinate the various parts of the secondary system, and eleven plus emerged under the contemporary pressures to extend the time spent by scholarship children in the secondary school.

One of Morant's main aims in developing a system of secondary schools was the improvement of the quality of teachers in the elementary schools. He saw the weakness of the progression from elementary school through a period as a pupil-teacher in an elementary school and back into teaching in an elementary school with for some, but not all, a period at training college. More than anything it was this inbred nature of the elementary teaching profession that Morant aimed to change. His policy was to substitute a liberal secondary education for at least some of the period spent as a pupil-teacher. From 1905 the new regulations laid down that pupil-teachers were to be sixteen and were to have had two years preparatory education, preferably in a secondary school. From 1907 bursaries were paid so that working-class children could afford to stay in full-time schooling. Initially the flow of teachers was disturbed since the new mode of entry decreased the numbers of working-class adolescents who wanted to teach. Few were willing to wait until sixteen to become pupil-teachers. On the other hand, there was no counter-balancing increase of middle-class entrants, as teaching was not yet an attractive enough profession to this social class. Yet new entrants had the chance of a fuller training in that the 1902 Act enabled the L.E.A.s to establish their own training colleges, and by 1914 there were twenty-two such colleges in addition to the denominational colleges. The war disrupted expansion since a large number of men enlisted, though to some extent women students took their place. By 1938 there were 83 colleges of which 54 were voluntary and 29 run by L.E.A.s. These colleges trained about 5,000 teachers per year of whom two-thirds were women. In addition the University Departments of Education were producing about 1,500 graduates from a four-year course combining degree work in academic subjects with the practice and theory of teaching.[1]

The quality of the elementary teaching profession did improve. By 1921 more than 85 per cent of intending teachers had undergone some secondary education. At this same date 1·3 per cent of elementary teachers were graduates; by 1938 this figure had risen to 7·3 per cent. Almost all elementary teachers had by then been trained as teachers, though more than half of secondary teachers had not. In the late twenties the decision was finally taken to discontinue the pupil-teacher method of training teachers that Kay-Shuttleworth had begun more than eighty years before. The L.E.A.s opposed this move, because they felt the pupil-teacher system tied students to them and gave working-class students a chance to know whether they were fitted to teach. In view of this opposition the Board allowed L.E.A.s to continue this mode of entry but ceased to pay grants for pupil-teachers. Their numbers fell rapidly.

The quality of instruction in the training colleges likewise improved. This was partly due to the higher quality of the entrants

[1] See A. Shakoor, *passim.*

since from soon after the war a majority had secondary education, but, in addition, these higher entry qualifications demanded a higher quality of college lecturer. By 1914 nearly three-quarters of L.E.A. college lecturers and almost two-thirds of lecturers in voluntary colleges were graduates; it can be seen that the new municipal colleges were starting to set the pace. Less attention had now to be given to the general education of entrants and more attention was given to the special subjects that the teacher wanted to teach and to professional education. New teaching methods, particularly for younger children, were based on the work of Montessori and of Dewey. The study of child development became central to the work of the colleges. Many of the colleges were still small and also often, particularly in the case of the voluntary colleges, residential. The process of moulding the teacher into the type that the colleges thought right was therefore very much easier. This was probably desirable socially if the contemporary style of teaching was not to be disrupted, but in many cases the result may very well have been detrimental to the personality development of the individual concerned.

In the early part of the century there was much discussion of linking the universities and the training colleges, since more graduates were going into teaching and the University Departments of Education were growing. Also it was felt that the universities should replace as examiners the Board of Education which was then responsible for most of the examining in the colleges. In 1925 a departmental committee reported in favour of some such link. Negotiations between groups of colleges and local universities enabled the Board to stop examining in 1929. This new link with the universities gave the colleges far more freedom to plan their own syllabuses.

The number of university enrolments rose both absolutely and proportionately throughout this period. In 1900–1 with a total population of 39 millions, 37,189 enrolled. But the various faculties grew at different rates. By 1938–9 arts enrolments had risen by 130 per cent, medicine by 100 per cent, pure science by 75 per cent and technology by only 20 per cent. In fact, the number of degrees awarded in science was falling in the late thirties.[1] Very valuable research was undertaken in the universities at this time. In the pure sciences the advances in physics that have led to atomic power were begun; in applied science important work in rubber technology and metallurgy was undertaken; in economics (Lord) Keynes made the theoretical formulations that underpin modern full employment policies; in the arts F. R. Leavis gave a new direction to literary criticism which ultimately had a profound social effect in making for a more critical awareness of such environmental influences as advertising and the mass media. But during the inter-war period much of the finance that enabled the universities to grow and do research came from the U.S.A. On occasion the Carnegie Fund donated more in one year than came from the British government in the same period. The Rockefeller Foundation enabled both Oxford and Cambridge Universities to rebuild their libraries and gave a substantial sum to London University for its new headquarters. Britain's entry into the modern university era was helped forward by the U.S.A.

Though the universities were not by the definition of 1902 part of the educational system, they were coming to have links with the state. Before the war the Board of Education had paid a grant to the universities. In 1911 a committee investigated the system; at the time the sum involved was only about £150,000 per year. The war disrupted university finance because income from fees fell. In 1919 a system akin to that recommended prior to the war was established. The University Grants Committee was set up to distribute monies granted by the Treasury. It acted as a buffer between the Treasury and the universities so as to guard the academic freedom of the latter. In 1919 the year's grant was raised to £1 million.

A number of research councils were established during this period. In 1916 the Department of Industrial and Scientific Research (D.S.I.R.) was set up as a result of the realization under the impact of the war with Germany that this country was lagging in its application of science to industry. In 1919 the Medical Research Council was established, and in 1931 the

[1] V. G. Couch, op. cit., pp. 190–3, quoting University Grants Committee Reports.

Agricultural Research Council followed. The research effort of these bodies was controlled by committees on which representatives of both the universities and industrial or professional bodies were members. Thus, though the work was done both in the universities and in specialized separate research institutes, one of the main functions of the universities was in some measure passing out of their complete control. The difficulty of maintaining the boundaries between educational institutions in such circumstances can be judged by the fact that from the late 1920s the D.S.I.R. began to train research students in chemistry and engineering to fill a further gap in supply left by the universities.

In some ways the 1902 Act had a detrimental effect on technical education as finance was diverted to the development of the secondary schools and teacher training. Yet this was a logical necessity since the clamour for technical education in the 1880s had blinded those in power to the need to establish good secondary schools upon which to base a sound system of technical education. Certainly by the early part of the century the lower levels of technical education were more soundly based on the teaching of the schools. The Board of Education wished to extend to the technical colleges the tolerance that it was giving to the schools. Around 1910 plans were made to discontinue the old science examinations originally run by the Department of Science and Art and also to stop the higher grade of City and Guild examinations. The intention was that colleges would step in to develop courses answering local industrial needs. This policy was a failure, and in the 1920s the City and Guilds took back responsibility for its higher examinations. In addition the Board of Education inaugurated the present system of National Certificates. These examinations were jointly organized by the Board, professional associations, and the colleges. The first Certificate in Mechanical Engineering was established in 1923. This system was a success and other Certificates in applied sciences were established, all based on a partnership between industry and education. During this period the links between industry and technical education were growing somewhat stronger, as firms donated equipment to colleges and as industrialists sat on various relevant committees.

The Conservative President of the Board in the late 1920s was Lord Eustace Percy, an enthusiast for technical education. He tried to do much, but was forced once again by economic circumstances to remain a publicist. His plans, like those of Fisher and those for the reorganization of secondary education, foundered on the need for national economy. Furthermore, it was difficult for industrialists to concentrate on developing technical education at a time when almost all their energies were spent in avoiding bankruptcy.

In brief, during the period up to 1914 resources were moving into education to meet the goals of the 1902 Act. This was particularly the case at the secondary stage. Great freedom was given to teachers to develop the schools as they wished, but the common assumption of H.M.I.s, those in power at the Board and headmasters forced the schools into a perpetuation of the class-bound system of the nineteenth century. After the war recurrent economic difficulties hindered rapid development. The educational system was by now more differentiated, since school welfare services and new types of post-primary schools were evolving. The pattern of the system was maintained by a supply of teachers that was improved in both quantity and quality. But the curriculum of educational institutions at every level up to the universities was slow to react to the new needs of the economy. Up to 1914 the chances that a unitary educational system would develop fairly rapidly seemed good, but these chances and the attempted redefinition of the post-war years disappeared in the despair of the inter-war years.

2 Strains

The last quarter of the nineteenth century was marked by considerable economic difficulty for Britain. There was some growth throughout this period, but there was also much unemployment and trading conditions were uncertain. From about 1896 there was an improvement and this lasted almost till the outbreak of war in 1914. This change for the better probably lulled those responsible for industrial and commercial enterprises into a false feeling that the worst was over and further major economic change was not needed. The war hit Britain hard and before recovery was achieved a series of grave economic crises began. The post-war inflation had come to an end by late 1919 and soon the government found it necessary to appoint the Geddes Committee to consider ways of economizing. This reported in 1922 and expenditure on education was seen as one likely source of economy.

One side-effect of the high wages during the war had been to increase the demand for education in the new L.E.A. fee-paying secondary schools. Slump conditions did not seem to diminish this newly created demand to its former level. In 1924 the Board of Education commented that there were cumulative changes 'working silently and unsuspected beneath the surface'.[1] The result was that a slowly rising demand for education met a policy of economy imposed by the government due to adverse economic conditions. This impasse occurred again after the improved trading period from 1924 to 1929 when an even worse slump began. Again, a committee was appointed and in 1933 the May Committee reported; once more the recommended cuts in expenditure severely hit the educational service.

During the inter-war years foreign competition was particularly severe and there was considerable reassessment of methods in industry. One change was that industrialists began to doubt the British tradition of amateurism. The Germans and Americans, two of our main industrial rivals, had for a long time put great faith in professional industrial managers. Though 'practical men' were still in much demand, some British industrialists came to see a need for employing scientifically trained men. New professional bodies were established; thus amongst others the Institute of Production Engineers was established in 1921 and the Institute of Chemical Engineers in 1922. Simultaneously, there grew up a strong belief in the necessity for research in industry. The number of American companies that invested in Britain encouraged these changes. General Motors/Vauxhall (1926) and Ford (1929) came during the twenties, Monsanto (1930) and Hoover (1931) in the early thirties. The average size of manufacturing unit was growing throughout this period. For all these reasons a new type of

[1] Board of Education Report, 1923–4, p. 23.

manager was wanted for whom a longer education, particularly of a scientific nature, was more important. This more professional group at the top of industry demanded a larger number of well-educated high-grade technicians and clerks to support it in administering the more complex industrial and commercial structure. This latter need affected education in two ways. Firstly, there was the demand from employers for more ex-grammar school boys with 'matric.', a qualification that guaranteed a minimum level of competence. Secondly, there was a demand from parents for secondary schooling, since they realized that the jobs to which 'matric.' could lead were those that were more secure, having a lower unemployment rate in slumps. In 1931 30·5 per cent of unskilled manual workers were unemployed, 14·4 per cent of skilled and semi-skilled manual workers, but only 5·5 per cent of clerks.

The difficult economic conditions had an effect on another social institution, the family. The birth-rate which had begun to drop in the 1870s fell very rapidly, until during the thirties the population of Britain was simply not reproducing itself. 61 per cent of women married in 1870–9 had five or more children, but only 4 per cent of those married in 1925 did so. Before long the population would clearly decline and, as a result, on the one hand labour would be short and on the other there would be a surplus supply of school places in the future. This did not help those who favoured a policy of expanding the school system. In addition, smaller families provided a totally different quality of experience for children, who missed the peer group experience that larger families could provide. However, several agencies of informal education became important during this period. Baden-Powell's first scout camp was held in 1907. By 1910 there were 109,000 Boy Scouts in Britain alone, and soon afterwards the Girl Guides were founded. Another educative agency that reached right into the family was set up soon after the war, namely the British Broadcasting Corporation, which dates from 1922. The radio soon became a powerful influence for the informal education of young and old alike, and its potentialities in formal education were recognized by the establishment of a system of broadcasts for schools.

In 1918 women came nearer to equality with men, when those over twenty-eight were given the vote; in 1928 the age for voting became the same for men and women. Political equality once achieved, women soon demanded economic equality; more particularly they began agitation for equal pay, especially in such professions as teaching. At this time women teachers were almost all unmarried, since at a time of great unemployment L.E.A.s operated a policy of giving a teacher her notice as soon as she married on the grounds that her husband could now support her and to keep her in work would possibly deprive an unemployed and deserving teacher of a job. It was impossible in the thirties to be a wife and a teacher.

The prominence for education of religion as an institution declined during the inter-war years. Attendance figures at churches, except for the Roman Catholic, fell considerably. The traditionally close link between family and religion grew weaker, as can be seen in the growing tendency to consider sending children to Sunday School as merely a convention rather than as a duty. Paradoxically this change in the importance of religion gave greater opportunity to those who wished to retain the dual system, since their opponents had now come to care less about the church schools. There were still those in positions of power who could make use of this new indifference. Such men could be found both in the Commons and the Lords. Some twenty bishops were members of the latter House, which still had considerable legislative powers.

For those who wished to keep religion a power in education the problem was the perennial one of raising sufficient finance. Up to 1902 the denominations had to help to provide a bare elementary education; by the 1930s the cry had risen for 'Secondary Education for All', and a reconstruction to this end had begun in which both sectors of the dual system had a part to play. This task proved rather easier for the Roman Catholics to achieve than for the Anglicans and other denominations. The number of Roman Catholic schools rose between 1900 and the outbreak of the second world war from 1,000 to 1,200 whilst the number of Anglican schools fell from 12,000 to 9,000.[1] There

[1] M. Cruickshank, op. cit., p. 141.

followed a shift in the emphasis of policy for all except the Catholics. Rather than stressing the retention of separate schools the denominations came to see that the best way of bringing religion to the children of the nation was to spread their influence throughout the state system. This new emphasis was to have effect on the 1944 Act.

When the reorganization of the post-elementary schools began after the late twenties administrative difficulties became apparent. Many of the denominational schools were too small to be run efficiently, but the churches were loath to give them up. Nor did they wish to lose the older children in their schools, though they found the task of raising money to build new secondary schools for such children beyond them. Quite clearly a redefinition of the situation was needed. In 1936 an Act was passed that formed the first major change in the 1902 religious settlement and by which the financial position of the various denominations was eased somewhat for the time being.

The passing of this Act is some measure of the contemporary indifference to religion, since though it did not go through both Houses unscathed, its passage was easy compared with that of the Act of 1902. The years immediately following the Balfour Act had been marked by much political strife over education. No amount of legal power can ensure the smooth operation of an educational system if the country or any part of it strongly objects; and in 1904 an Act had to be passed to force certain strongly nonconformist local authorities, mainly in Wales, to implement the 1902 Act. These authorities refused to subsidize from the rates religious institutions to which they were opposed. Many people hoped that the election of the Liberal government in 1906 would result in a new definition of the situation. However, the failure of Birrell's and Runciman's Acts in 1908 and the growing interest in other political matters left the 1902 Act unchanged.

The main political strain that was to become important during the inter-war years lay elsewhere, namely in the changing concept of social equality. In the 1900 election the Labour Party put candidates up for the first time in its own right; beforehand, their candidates had stood on the Liberal-Labour ticket.

At the 1906 election some thirty Labour M.P.s were returned. The ensuing period of Liberal rule up to 1914 was one marked by fierce political strife; one of the central issues was the reduction of social inequality. This was symbolized by the introduction of land taxes. The wealthy saw this as an attempt to force them to pay for such welfare measures as sickness and unemployment benefits which helped the poor; in fact these schemes were largely financed on the contributory principle.

One of the first results of this position was the issue by McKenna of the 1907 Free Place Regulations, the aim of which was 'to secure that all secondary schools aided by grants shall be made fully accessible to children of all classes'. Grammar schools who offered 25 per cent of their places free to former elementary school pupils could attract a higher grant from the Treasury. Fisher's Act of 1918 by raising the minimum leaving age to fourteen for all went a little way further to ensure that more working-class children might ascend the now wider rungs of the scholarship ladder. Good intentions were often spoilt by economic conditions, since it was often hard for a working-class family to send a child to school beyond fourteen at a time of heavy unemployment.

Gradually the definition of equality changed. In the pre-war era many people had seen a chance to gain a scholarship to the schools of the élite as equality, but there had been a minority who wished a more radical policy. From 1906 onwards the Trades Union Congress regularly passed a resolution demanding secondary education for all up to sixteen. In 1922 R. H. Tawney, a distinguished economic historian, wrote *Secondary Education for All*. His thoughts moved the now much stronger Labour Party towards the aim of a common secondary school. These changing views on equality also affected the Consultative Committee which in 1926 published a report under its chairman, Sir Henry Hadow, entitled *The Education of the Adolescent*. This report recommended a radical reorganization of post-elementary education. In 1934 the Trades Union Congress gave evidence in favour of a common secondary school to the Consultative Committee, then considering Secondary Education under Sir

Will Spens. The Spens Report of 1938 went further than the Hadow Report and recommended as an aim parity of esteem for all types of secondary school.

The outbreak of the war in 1939 checked action on the Spens Report. Some reorganization of higher elementary education along the lines outlined by the Hadow Report had taken place. By 1939 69 per cent of urban and 22 per cent of rural elementary schools had been reorganized so that the children of secondary age were no longer in all-age schools but were in separate schools catering solely for those over eleven. The slump had slowed down this process of reorganization. In addition, the May Committee had recommended in 1931 that Free Places be replaced by Special Places. Grants for these places were dependent upon parental income, thereby making more difficult the financial position of many working-class families whose children were capable of going to grammar school. The actual result of the changes in policy on the provision of more secondary education and particularly on increasing the chances of able working-class children of gaining entry to grammar school, was as follows: 27·0 per cent of middle-class and 4·0 per cent of working-class boys born between 1899 and 1910 had a secondary education, but the figures for those born between 1910 and 1929 had risen to 38·9 per cent and 9·8 per cent respectively. A wide social class differential still existed.[1]

Support for the Labour Party had grown considerably in the inter-war years, and there had been two minority Labour governments. The educational policy of this party was based on the new definition of equality even if economic conditions had prevented the policy from becoming reality. As more of the working class went to grammar school they came to see their education as more like that of the middle class; they too had a right to a secondary education. This meant, firstly, staying at school longer than the minimum leaving age and, secondly, a system of schools that could really be called 'secondary'. It was hoped to gain the first aim by raising the school-leaving age to

---

[1] J. E. Floud, 'The Educational Experience of the Adult Population of England and Wales as at July, 1949', in D. V. Glass (editor), *Social Mobility in Britain*, London, 1954.

fifteen. The Hadow reorganization hoped to achieve the second aim by creating senior schools distinct from the old elementary schools. Depressed conditions strengthened the working class in their plea for entry to secondary education because the jobs to which the grammar schools led were those that were most secure at the time. Education was seen to be instrumental in gaining status and security, but was also difficult to achieve for the members of a social class that had low wages and, on average, larger families.

The middle class was coming to accept that the working class should have a greater chance of secondary education, but had not made any change in the definition of its own education. The political pressure for equality had not led to marked criticism of the public schools; the élite were still to be educated apart. Hence, though the grammar school was to be more open to the working class it was still seen as a school for the lower élite and entry for a working-class child was seen as a privilege rather than a right. The Spens Committee did consider the possibility of 'multilateral schools', in which all types of secondary education would be undertaken together, but despite some advantages 'reluctantly decided . . . not (to) advocate as a general policy the substitution of such multilateral schools for separate schools of the existing types'. The arguments that swung the issue were based mainly on tradition and administrative convenience.[1]

Despite the pressure for an enlarged educational system the proportion of the national income devoted to education did not rise during the period. In 1922 public expenditure on education was 2·4 per cent of net national income; in 1932 the proportion was 2·6 per cent, but by 1939 the figure had fallen to 2·2 per cent.[2] There were, nevertheless, considerable developments within education itself. The shortage of teachers that was apparent in 1900 was aggravated by the changes in methods of entry that Morant initiated. The first world war disrupted supply, and Fisher's Act in 1918 created further demands for teachers. Clearly some action was needed to make teaching more attractive, and the National Union of Teachers used its growing

[1] *Secondary Education*, 1938, pp. xix–xxi.
[2] J. Vaizey, *The Costs of Education*, 1959, p. 76.

strength to gain better working conditions for its members. The 1918 Superannuation Act gave the teachers a non-contributory pension scheme, though this scheme was changed in 1925 into a contributory one. In 1919 the teachers were very dissatisfied with their salary scales. There was at that time no one national scale, and the National Union of Teachers initiated strike action in some of the areas where rates of pay were very much below the national averages. Fisher established three committees on pay. These were committees for elementary, secondary and technical teachers. Lord Burnham was chairman of all three. Negotiations led to standard scales agreeable to all Local Education Authorities. This award ran out in 1925 when the Burnham Committee met again to make a further award. In 1926 the Board issued Regulations making the awards of this committee compulsory in all areas. The new negotiating machinery ended much exploitation of teachers, but it built into the salary scale the existing definition of education since there were separate elementary and secondary scales.

The academic study of education became much more widespread during this period and began to have some influence on the practice of the schools. This was particularly true in the case of educational psychology. There were two important sources of influence. Firstly, there was that associated with the growing interest in the measurement of abilities. During the first decade of the century Binet had done pioneer work in this field in Paris. As early as 1913 (Sir) Cyril Burt was appointed as psychologist to the London County Council; his work together with that of such other British psychologists as Spearman and Godfrey Thompson was to have a great impact especially on the development of tests for selection of children for grammar schools. Soon after the war Northumberland and Bradford adopted group administered tests of mental ability for their scholarship examinations, and they were followed by other Local Education Authorities. Clearly this growth encouraged the demand for more exact selection for secondary education. The importance given to psychology can be judged by the fact that in 1938 the Spens Report contained a chapter on the bodily and mental development of children between eleven and sixteen.

The development of this new branch of educational study was reflected in the curricula of the training colleges, but a second source of the influence of psychology was of equal importance. This sprang from the studies of behaviour made initially by such American psychologists as Macdougal. Later this interest in behaviour was, however, much influenced by work stemming from the psychoanalytical thought of Freud, Jung and Adler. As a result of these trends a great interest in child behaviour and development was born. This had much influence on the teaching methods used, especially with younger children. These more child-centred techniques were greatly at odds with the old elementary school tradition that put so much stress on the child learning merely the three R's and sitting still at his desk. This change can be seen in the 1937 Handbook for Teachers which emphasized the importance of the personal relationships between the teacher and the child and went as far as to comment on 'the gradual recognition on the part of teachers that the superiority of the adult over the child is a matter of length and width of experience and not of moral ability'.[1] The role of teacher was becoming very different from that in the nineteenth century.

The growing importance of the various strains described here can be seen in reports of the Consultative Committee published during the inter-war years. These were the Hadow Reports on *The Education of the Adolescent* (1926), *The Primary School* (1931), *The Nursery School* (1933), and the Spens Report on *Secondary Education* (1938). The two reports on schools for the younger child were influenced by the new methods of teaching. Thus, the Hadow Report of 1931 spoke of 'primary' education, in itself a new term that had a very different flavour from the traditional 'elementary'. The committee saw the main task of the primary school as being the provision to children between seven and eleven of 'what is essential to their healthy growth – physical, intellectual and moral'; the curriculum was 'to be thought of in terms of activity and experience rather than knowledge to be acquired and facts to be stored'.[2] This redefinition was

[1] Op. cit., p. 88.
[2] *The Primary School*, 1931, pp. 92–3.

clearly a direct, though a much more liberal, descendant of Morant's 1904 Elementary Code.

The two reports on secondary schools were more influenced by the changing definition of equality. Thus, the Hadow Report *The Education of the Adolescent* recommended that 'between the age of eleven and (if possible) that of fifteen, all . . . who do not go forward to "secondary education" in the present narrow sense of the word, should go forward none the less to what is, in our view, a form of secondary education, in the truer and broader sense of the word'. The term 'elementary' was to be abolished and there were to be two stages to schooling, primary and secondary. The new wider secondary education was to be given mainly in either the already existing grammar schools or in the envisaged modern schools, in which 'the courses of instruction, though not merely vocational or utilitarian, should be used to connect the school work with interests arising from the social and industrial environment of the pupils'.[1]

The Hadow Report had cleared the ground for the Spens Committee to build on; the political demand for a more egalitarian secondary system had deeply impressed itself on these documents. The Spens Report recommended free secondary education for all in a tripartite system consisting of equal Grammar, Modern and Technical High Schools. Most significant of all, the term 'elementary' was to be abolished. In place of two parallel codes, one of higher and one of lower status, there were to be two stages, primary and secondary, between which status differences would be irrelevant. It was upon these four reports that the massive redefinition of the 1944 Act was to be based.

3 Redefinition

On 1 September 1939 the minimum school-leaving age should have been raised at long last to fifteen. This proved impossible since war broke out on 3 September. The immediate effect of war was educational chaos, since children were evacuated from densely populated urban areas because of the fear of heavy bombing. The schools in both urban and rural areas were greatly disrupted. The ultimate result was that many who had not known

[1] *The Education of the Adolescent*, 1926, pp. xxi–xxiii, and 175.

the educational state of the country were jolted into a truer knowledge. As in the first world war idealism was kindled to start planning the post-war reconstruction. There was one big difference, however, between the preparations for the 1944 Act and any plan made before. The idea of consultation had by now penetrated deeply into the framework of government. In 1941 the wartime Coalition government sent out The Green Book, a long questionnaire seeking views on the many aspects of educational reconstruction from the groups and persons who were considered to be rightful bodies to advise those in power. R. A. Butler was appointed President of the Board and embarked on a strenuous round of negotiations with all concerned and particularly with the churches. Butler gave much thought to the problems of the dual system, but he judged that it was not possible to ignore the long-established position of the denominations in the provision of education. Half the schools in the country were still church schools of one denomination or another. Furthermore, unlike many people who claimed to be interested in education the churches had a clear educational policy. After long negotiation Butler reached a compromise with all the interested denominations. This was no ideal solution, but it was politically possible and all concerned had a stake in making it work.

In 1943 Butler gave an account of the replies received to The Green Book. The consensus of opinion was for one code, an end to the elementary code, secondary education for all, the abolition of fees in all secondary schools, the raising of the minimum school-leaving age to fifteen immediately and to sixteen as soon as possible, and for compulsory part-time education up to eighteen for those not otherwise in school. The government issued a White Paper, *Educational Reconstruction*, which formed the basis for the drafting of the new Act.

The 1944 Education Act was a truly massive redefinition. Butler's aim was to build a unified system to meet all the recent strains, but one that had as far as possible some continuity with what went before. The redefinitions of the reports of the thirties were influential, though not always explicitly so. The important switch from codes to stages was clear: 'The statutory system . . .

102

shall be organized in three progressive stages to be known as primary education, secondary education, and further education.' [1] The word 'elementary' was cut out of the educational vocabulary.

Secondary education was to be for all and free. Yet there was no definite legislation on how the secondary schools were to be organized. The assumed definition of the situation was that there should be a tripartite system as the Spens Report had recommended. This method had received further approval from the Norwood Committee on *The Curriculum and Examinations in Secondary Schools* whose report was published in 1943, ten days after the White Paper on Educational Reconstruction. This report found psychological justification for a system of secondary organization that was fundamentally based on historical development and on social attitudes that had been stronger in the pre-1914 period than in the 1930s. The committee considered that there were three different types of mind that fitted the suggested three types of school. Firstly, those who were 'interested in learning for its own sake', and who could 'grasp an argument or follow a piece of connected reasoning' were destined for the grammar school. Next, children 'whose interests and abilities lie markedly in the field of applied science or applied art' were suited to a technical school. The very wording used is reminiscent of the late nineteenth century and of the low status attributed then to technical education. Lastly, some who dealt 'more easily with concrete things than with ideas' would best continue their education in a modern school. [2] These remarks were based on a psychology that was already considered rather doubtful, but the recommendations of the report were nevertheless influential in determining what sort of secondary education for all should be given within the range of tolerance permitted by the Act.

At the level of tertiary education, technical and further education were defined into the Act, and full consultations were held with various interested bodies such as the Trades Union

[1] Education Act, 1944, Part II, 7.

[2] *Report on Curriculum of Secondary Schools and Examinations*, 1943, pp. 2–3.

Congress and the Federation of British Industries. Again the Act did not specify exact details of the way in which the system should develop. The training colleges were also subsumed under the legislation either through the Local Authorities or the denominations. In 1944 the very important McNair Report on *Teachers and Youth Leaders* was published. This recommended the establishment under the aegis of each university of an Institute of Education to be responsible for all teacher training, and in all cases except that of Cambridge such a reorganization followed. It should be noted that, although the proportion of the parliamentary grant in annual university expenditure had risen from 23 per cent in 1920 to 28 per cent in 1940 and the yearly total of these monies had risen from £4·2 millions to £8·6 millions over this same period,[1] the universities were not included in the 1944 Act. However, in 1946 the terms of reference of the University Grants Committee were expanded to make sure that the universities were fully able to meet national needs.

One of the biggest changes made by the Act was in respect of religious instruction in the schools. The system of agreed syllabuses was to continue, but religious instruction was to be compulsory in all Local Education Authority schools. Religious instruction could now be taught at any time in the school day, not only in the first or last period, so that opting out became more difficult. These conditions were also to apply to controlled schools, namely those originally provided by denominations but now wholly financed by the Local Education Authority. In general the denominational schools received very favourable financial terms; and in the case of controlled schools it could be said that denominational religious instruction could not be given in what were virtually state schools.

As a final symbol of the great changes made by the Butler Act the old Board of Education was abolished and a Ministry was established. After the passage of the Act in August 1944 Butler became the first Minister of Education that this country had appointed. It is of interest to note that by the 1899 Act the exact composition of the Board of Education had been laid down, but that between 1902 and 1944 this Board never actually met.

[1] J. Vaizey, op. cit., p. 200.

4 Conclusion

The 1902 Act did much to coordinate the educational effort of the country and led to an expansion of the resources devoted to education especially at the secondary level. This growth was checked by the outbreak of war in 1914. Despite the hopes of many, Fisher did not spark off further growth after the war, mainly because the inter-war years were marked by severely depressed economic conditions. The pre-war expansion was not brought about by Acts, but by the issue of regulations within the range of tolerance permitted by the 1902 Act and depending upon the developing contemporary definition of education. The work of Morant was basic to the direction of the development of the English educational system after 1902. Very important for the problem of coordinating the system was the trend towards further differentiation and particularly into such welfare activities as the meals and medical services. An especially noteworthy development was in the field of teacher training, where changes in the methods of recruitment and training raised the quality of teachers and hence the whole tone of the elementary system.

By the 1930s the definition implicit in the 1902 Act did not meet contemporary political, economic and educational opinion. Political changes of power symbolized by the rise of the Labour Party demanded a more egalitarian educational system. Economic conditions had forced Britain to face severe foreign competition. There was a growing realization that a more professional approach to industry and commerce was needed and must largely rest on a firm basis of scientific and technical education at every level, but particularly at the university level where the status of such subjects was low. One result of this was the establishment of special research councils outside, though to some extent influenced by, the universities whose expansion raised problems of the exact boundaries of the educational system.

Change of a purely educational nature had also led to strains. The growing expertise in educational psychology was a help in the attempts to make entry to grammar school fairer, but the move towards a more child-centred mode of teaching was at odds with the elementary tradition. This latter strain was reflected in the Hadow Report of 1931 on *The Primary School* whose title was in itself a mark of a changing emphasis at the first stage of education. The position of the Consultative Committee had become crucial since it represented a built-in agency of highly informed and progressive, as opposed to avant-garde, criticism of the system. This Committee constantly worked for redefinition of education at whatever level was under consideration. The Hadow Report of 1926 on *The Education of the Adolescent* gave the direction for whatever secondary reorganization was possible in the thirties.

For the religious denominations this reorganization meant more financial stringency. Yet, because there was on the whole indifference towards religion, the influence of the denominations could be greater. Attempts to aid the church schools led to the temporary and rather *ad hoc* redefinition of the 1936 Act, by which a new type of school, the Special Agreement school, was created in order to channel more money to the denominations. The outbreak of war in 1939 brought this age of despair to an end. Very soon plans were begun to redefine education. Under the able political guidance of R. A. Butler the 1944 Act was passed in a spirit of hope and with far less animosity than the Acts of 1870 and 1902.

CHAPTER FIVE

TOWARDS A FAIR SYSTEM

The despair of the inter-war years had hit education hard, but new hope was born in the war and the 1944 Act was rightly heralded as the dawn of a new educational era. The definitions that were explicit and implicit in the overall redefinition were marked more by the attempt to be fair than by any other single aim. But detailed implementation was as usual left to occur within the range of tolerance permitted by the legislation, and the assumptions reigning among those in power in the government and the Ministry in the late forties were based on what advanced thought of the thirties had considered fairness to be. Very soon after the war the idea of what was meant by 'fair' began to change. Educational policies based on this new thinking were soon formulated. As a result the organization of the system as it was developing came in for much criticism. In particular, the mode of selection for and organization of secondary education were constant topics for private discussion and public pronouncements.

The post-war years were marked by a new type of economic crisis. In the late 1930s Keynes had shown how to avoid mass unemployment. All parties in the war-time Coalition government supported a White Paper issued in 1944 on full employment policy. Heavy unemployment was ended, but apparently only at the cost of inflation, and the attempts to cure this new ill were hampered by the slow realization of just how many of our profitable overseas investments had been sold in order to win the war. Thus there was a constant danger of trying to over-employ our scarce resources. The problem had changed from that of scarcity to that of how to allocate our more plentiful resources. How much extra was education to have and within the educational sector how much was each branch of the service to have?

In the two decades after the second world war there was much qualitative change and great quantitative growth in English education. Despite a movement towards a fairer system by the criterion of equal chances of entry to grammar school for each social class, there was an increasing strain between education and political institutions because this greater equality no longer met many people's definition of fairness. Furthermore, the constant stress on economic problems led to a reassessment of the links between educational and economic institutions. These two strains were very influential in the reports of the Central Advisory Committee, successor to the Consultative Committee, in this period. A series of these reports containing many recommendations brought the system near to the threshold of a further massive redefinition by the late 1960s.

1 Growth

The administration of education had become more centralized as a result of the 1944 Act. The number of L.E.A.s had been reduced from 315 to about half that number. Each authority found on average just under half of the finance it needed for the provision of education whilst the Treasury found the rest. Though the greater power lay with the centre, each L.E.A. had considerable power to decide details to suit local demands and conditions. With the growth of the child population and the general expansion of the educational services education soon became the major single responsibility of local government, particularly at a time when many of their former responsibilities such as hospitals, electricity and gas, were handed over to national bodies.

The new Act laid down that each L.E.A. had to appoint an Education Officer. He acted as the chief executive officer of the

Education Committee and could do much to shape policy by the expert advice given to his lay committee. It had become the rule to recruit such administrators from former teachers. By the 1940s this had also come to be the case for H.M.I.s. Thus both those in administrative power locally and the Inspectorate, who acted as the eyes and ears of the Minister and his civil servants, were recruited from former teachers. This method of recruitment ensured that the civil servants knew the day-to-day problems of the schools, but it also meant that any development that differed greatly from the current beliefs and assumptions of teachers, might possibly be hampered at both administrative and school levels.

The ending of the elementary code released a great head of energy. This was very true in the new primary schools, which were by the Act to have parity of esteem with secondary schools. As a symbol of this in 1945 the first Burnham award after the Act put all teachers on the same salary scale, though, because graduate status attracted further increments and there were more graduates in secondary schools, average salaries were still lower in primary schools. Another reason for lower rewards in these schools was that the majority of the teachers were women, whose pay scale was lower than that of men. However, this cause was soon eliminated since by stages over a period women teachers came to have equal pay with men.

Between 1945 and 1965 about 5,000 new primary schools have been built, providing 1·2 million places, and another 0·8 million places have been created by extensions and remodelling. Yet in 1962 0·7 million primary children, 19 per cent of the total, were in schools where the oldest main building dated from before 1875. The majority of schools still had outside sanitation. The building programme has encouraged two other changes. In 1949 36 per cent of thirteen-year-olds were in all-age schools, but by 1965 this figure had fallen to 1 per cent; this is one measure of the coming of a real primary stage to education. Secondly, in 1947 34 per cent of nine-year-olds were in single-sex schools, by 1965 only 3 per cent were; this move to co-education was one more facet of the move to equal treatment for all in the schools.[1]

[1] *Children and their Primary Schools*, 1967, pp. 98 and 389–90.

There was a great need to build new primary schools after the war for three reasons. Firstly, there were bombed schools to rebuild; secondly, there were old schools to replace; lastly, there were new schools needed for the sudden rise in the birth-rate. It was these new schools that set the pace in primary education. Architecturally they were of advanced design and educationally they tended to be experimental in atmosphere. The headmaster often was responsible for the creation of a permissive atmosphere, very different in spirit from that of the old elementary code. The role of the head was changing. According to the 1905 Handbook one of the head's duties had been to organize at regular intervals formal examinations of the school's work in the three R's. In the 1959 Handbook the head was described as 'an organizer of learning' who no longer necessarily taught one specific class. Far more attention came to be given to creativity by children in art, English and in physical activities. Education of the senses was now considered in many ways as important as the three R's. New teaching methods were tried. One stimulus here was the shortage of teachers. Many mechanical ways of learning were introduced into the schools; such were the use of programmed learning, of teaching machines and of television programmes.

Another influence in ways of teaching came from the continuing stress on educational psychology. More stress came to be put on rewards than on punishments, particularly among younger children. Though the majority of teachers still favoured the occasional use of corporal punishment, the use of such negative sanctions became rare in most primary schools. Part of the continued interest in psychology stemmed from the work done on scientific selection by the armed services, who had relied extensively on such methods for choosing their officers. After the war some of the results of this work and of the interest engendered were applied to selection of primary pupils for secondary grammar schools. This undoubtedly met the political demands for fairness, but had an important feedback effect on the primary schools. Infant methods were not affected, but in the majority of junior schools much effort was expended in achieving the maximum possible number of eleven plus successes.

110

This was done by giving pupils in the final year extensive practice in intelligence tests, in mental arithmetic and in the sorts of English work tested in attainment tests. Such training could hardly be called educative and ran counter to the more liberal methods already mentioned.

The 1944 Act had made secondary education free for all. Most people understood that the Act would be translated into administrative terms in such a way that there would be three types of secondary schools which would be given 'parity of esteem'. This was the policy of Spens and of the thirties. The Act rested on the meritocratic principle that all should have equality of opportunity, but in the setting of the tripartite system and the atmosphere of the post-war period 'equal chances' was interpreted as 'equal chances to enter the grammar school', which was clearly seen as the pathway to economic and hence usually to social status. The survival power of any social organization is largely determined by public support, and there was immense support for the grammar school.

The Labour Government elected in 1945 with a large majority set about creating the new secondary system and defined it in tripartite terms. However, there was opposition to this policy from a few urban areas where councils dominated by supporters of the Labour Party planned and began to build comprehensive schools that would recruit all the secondary pupils in their catchment areas except those who went to private schools. By the late fifties there was a proliferation of types of secondary system throughout the country. All aimed to increase the holding power of the schools so that more children were given a true secondary education and stayed beyond the minimum school-leaving age. This policy was based on grounds of both egalitarianism and of economic necessity, since more skilled manpower seemed necessary for economic survival. However, the grammar school did not disappear. Values usually change before the institutions that they support and once the underpinning values have changed it takes time to alter the organization that survives. Furthermore, those in favour of a reorganization of secondary education met intense opposition and only grew strong enough to influence national policy by the sixties.

One of the first results of the 1944 Act was the raising of the school-leaving age to fifteen from April 1947. Ellen Wilkinson, the Minister of Education, did this as an act of faith against the advice of countless Jeremiahs who foretold a shortage of teachers, classrooms and even of furniture. In each of these cases specific action was taken. Perhaps most successful was the Emergency Training Scheme to secure quickly as many teachers as possible. Many mature men and women were recruited on demobilization from the forces often with minimal academic qualification. These teachers attended intensive courses and during their probationary period went to further part-time courses. The majority of those trained in this unorthodox way proved capable teachers.

In the 1950s a bulge in the birth-rate added to the demand for places at first in primary schools and then in the secondary schools. There was also a trend for pupils to stay on at secondary school beyond the first school examination, now reorganized as the Ordinary Level of the General Certificate of Education (G.C.E.). The sixth forms of the grammar schools grew in size. Partly this was due to some middle-class parents transferring their custom from the private schools to the state system, but in the main this trend resulted from the rise in the educational standard demanded at the point of entry to the labour force. Another result of the increased importance of the link between education and the economy was that the weight given to classics in the curriculum became less and the demand for science and mathematics rose. The status of these subjects rose as education came to be seen as serving a more instrumental function. Yet the increase in secondary facilities was not spread equally over the country; in 1960 the proportion of seventeen-year-olds at school varied from 27·9 per cent in Cardiganshire to 2·5 per cent in Bury.[1]

Education at a grammar school was now free and yet the fee-paying public schools and the preparatory schools that served them flourished after the war. In 1942 the Fleming Committee in its report, *The Public Schools and the General Educational System*, had recommended some measure of integration with the state system. Despite experiments by several schools, little was achieved in this direction. The public schools remained much in

[1] *Higher Education*, Appx I, 1963, p. 65.

demand. There were several reasons for this. Perhaps sheer tradition is the most important; the British upper and middle classes had sent their children, especially their sons, to these schools for a century and saw no reason to change their ways. Certainly, these schools had excellent links with the universities and were able to place their pupils well, especially at the two older universities. This was crucial at a time when formal qualifications had become so important in either retaining or in gaining social position. More especially was this true for those entering industry and more ex-public school boys were doing so. Before the war this had not been the case. Industry had to some extent lost its stigma, though the cause of this may well have been the closing of such other outlets for the former pupils of these schools as the Indian Army and colonial civil service because of the move from Empire to Commonwealth. The greater emphasis on industrial careers had the same effect as in the grammar schools in strengthening the science, at the expense of the classical, sixth forms. Such adaptability enabled the public schools to retain their clientele.

Of the schools in the tripartite system the Secondary Technical School fared least well after 1945. There were 302 schools of this type in 1955, but only 172 by 1965; however, the number of pupils fell only from 87,366 to 84,587, indicating a great increase in size of Technical Schools.[1] The Spens and Norwood Committees had seen the Technical High School as one particular type of secondary school needed on educational grounds and wanted by parents on its merits. This situation changed in the 1950s. Since many of these schools had always recruited at thirteen plus, to parents whose children had failed the eleven-plus the Technical School was a second chance to save their children from what they saw as the stigma of the Modern School. Simultaneously, much of the pre-war function of the Technical School was lost to the two other types of school. The pressure for science and the more vocationally oriented subjects led the grammar school to teach, for instance, mechanical drawing, a subject in pre-war days considered to be right outside its normal curriculum. Meanwhile the pressure for formal

[1] *Statistics of Education*, Part I, 1965, p. 44.

educational qualifications to meet the needs of the work force led more and more secondary modern schools to provide the courses for the first external examinations which were formerly one of the attractions of the Technical School. Many of these schools became merged with either Modern or grammar schools in bilateral schools. Certainly, as a school type their importance diminished, but much of the approach that they typified is now very strong in the other existing secondary schools.

The Secondary Modern School was the hope of the 1944 Act in that this new type of school was the one to which the majority of the population would go and was the one that had to be given parity of esteem with the two other already existing types. Soon it was apparent that esteem cannot be given but must be earned. The Modern School recruited its pupils from parents of lower social class and fed its pupils into the lower ranks of the labour force. For both reasons it attracted lower status to itself than did the grammar or Technical School whose pupils were from higher status homes and went to higher status occupations. Head-masters of Modern Schools attempted to raise the prestige of their schools by moulding them in the image of the higher status schools. They organized their schools on the house system, had prefects, adopted school uniforms and entered a small, though growing, proportion of their pupils for the same examinations as the grammar schools. The very attempt to win prestige drew attention to their lower status.

So great was the demand in the Modern Schools for examinations that the Beloe Committee on Secondary School Examinations other than the G.C.E. was set up. This Committee reported in 1960 and recommended that a new system of examinations for the Certificate of Secondary Education (C.S.E.) be established to cater for the band of children covering those of average ability to those just able to sit Ordinary Level. This examination started in 1965 and was influenced by the drive towards less traditional methods of teaching and examination in the secondary schools. Thus both an internal examination with external moderation and the inclusion of a large proportion of course work in place of a traditional terminal examination were possible in C.S.E.

The Modern Schools also put stress on such extracurricular activities as clubs and school games. However, one development that has influenced all secondary schools is relevant here. There has been increasing interest in individual as opposed to team sports and in the more informal as opposed to formal physical activities. Such team games as football and cricket are still very popular, but there has been a great rise in the interest shown in, for example, mountaineering and canoeing. This greater individualism has also been apparent in the way that physical education has been taught to older boys and girls. Physical jerks have gone and have been replaced, for instance, by a series of individual physical exercises for boys and modern dance or free movement for girls. Youth no longer will be dragooned into conformity, but wants to show individuality. Symbolic of this change has been the foundation of the Duke of Edinburgh's Award based on reaching agreed standards of excellence in groups of very varied physical and intellectual activities and with an emphasis on service to others. All types of school, including apprenticeship schools run by industrial enterprises, have shown increasing interest in this scheme and adolescents have supported this interest.

During the decade between 1955 and 1965 the numbers of Modern Schools rose slowly from 3,550 with 1·2 million pupils to 3,727 with 1·6 million pupils. Once again the average size of school rose. However, the main growth in the secondary field was in the number of comprehensive schools in answer to the demands for greater equality of educational opportunity. In 1955 there was 16 such schools with 15,891 pupils; by 1965 there were 262 with 239,619 pupils. 77 of these schools were in the London area.[1] Comprehensive schools were an answer to political pressure in urban areas, but often met economic needs in such rural areas as Westmorland or Anglesey. In these sparsely populated areas full secondary education for all with adequate facilities for a sixth form could only be provided by centralizing provision so that scarce resources of finance and of teachers were used economically.

The egalitarian pressures so obviously at work on the way the

[1] *Statistics of Education*, Part I, 1965, p. 44.

schools developed also encouraged the growth of ancillary services. By the 1944 Act the School Medical Service became known as the School Health Service. The money spent on this service increased from 1955 to 1965 at a more rapid rate than expenditure on straightforward educational provision. The same was the case for Special Schools for physically and mentally handicapped children. There were other forces at work. In 1939 the Youth Service had been established due to a feeling of greater social responsibility for the leisure time activities of youth. There was a rapid growth of resources spent in this field in the decade up to 1965 partly to meet the needs of adolescents who became defined as a major problem group in the more wealthy society of post-war Britain.

Economic forces were also important in the growth of ancillary services since there was a need to avoid any loss of talent by ensuring that young persons found jobs as near their capabilities as possible. As a result of the Employment and Training Act of 1948 the Youth Employment Service was reorganized. L.E.A.s could opt to run this service for their own areas and 129 did so out of a total possible of about 150. Between 1950 and 1956 the number of Youth Employment Officers was static around 770, but by 1965 there were 1,340.[1] This great increase was mainly necessary to cope with the movement into work of the children born as a result of the post-war rise in the birth-rate.

Despite the apparent immense needs of the economy, technical education was the area of the slowest growth in the first decade after the war. Employers seemed only slowly to realize its growing importance. This tendency was visible both in the slow growth of use of the technical colleges and in the failure of implementation of the sections of the 1944 Act that dealt with the County Colleges. Fisher's vision of part-time education for young workers was once again written into the legislation, but was only to be implemented when possible. So far day release of this nature has not been given a high enough priority to be made compulsory. Yet there has been an increase in the number of youths under eighteen released by employers in this way.

Fundamentally technical education still had low status. As

[1] *The Future Development of the Youth Employment Service*, 1965, p. 41.

late as 1956 a member could still say in parliament that technical education is 'definitely "servants' hall", if not "scullery", whereas academic education is "dining room" or "upstairs" '.[1] But it was in this year that the government issued a White Paper on which a reorganization was based, and as a result of which the second post-war decade has been marked by a great expansion in the facilities given to this branch of education. Between 1955 and 1965 current expenditure on all further education quadrupled and capital expenditure rose more than threefold.

A rapid expansion in the numbers taking National Certificate and City and Guilds courses occurred. Furthermore the proportion who did these courses full-time rather than part-time rose, and this was a useful change from the tradition of night school since wastage rates at part-time evening classes are very high. Yet the symbol of this great growth was the establishment of technological universities akin to the German Technische Hochschule. This development had been recommended in 1945 in the Report on Higher Technological Education of a committee whose chairman was Lord Percy. There was a small number of technical colleges in Britain of a very high academic standard where students had for some time been prepared for London University external degrees even to doctorial level. This growth had occurred for various reasons. There has been a tendency for technical education to perform a residual function, picking up the tasks that other sections of the educational system were unable to do. In the post-war period when the universities were unable to expand as rapidly as was necessary these colleges could take up some of the demand for highly qualified manpower, with the result that by 1956 they were designated as Colleges of Advanced Technology. This position was changed when the government acted on the recommendations made in the Robbins Report on Higher Education in 1963, as a result of which a new British type of educational institution of university status was created, namely the technological university.

Another fast-growing sector of higher education in the second post-war decade was the training of teachers. As has been

[1] *Hansard*, 5th Series, Vol. 554, Col. 1698.

117

indicated, this development was necessary to meet the rising child population in the schools. Another need was to replace the very high rate of wastage among young women teachers who married much earlier than before the war. After 1939 these women did not have to leave the profession, but they soon wanted to do so in order to have children. In the early 1960s 19,000 teachers per year joined the schools, but 18,000 left. In 1938–9 there had been 13,000 students in teacher training establishments in Britain. By 1956 this figure had doubled and there were 26,000; in the next decade the total doubled again and by 1965 there were 62,286 students on initial training courses.[1] As a result of the important recommendations made in 1944 by the McNair Committee the universities in almost the whole country had become responsible through Institutes of Education for organizing the training of teachers. This administrative measure brought the colleges into closer contact with university staff in arranging syllabuses and in the setting and marking of examinations. This had a positive effect on the colleges' standards and courses. However, one other major recommendation of the McNair Report was not followed until 1960, namely the lengthening of the period of training from two to three years. When this change was made the Ministry of Education commented that 'the conscious aim . . . [was] to foster an academic and social life in the colleges more akin to that of the universities'.[2]

The innovation which went furthest to give the colleges a position more akin to the universities was a result of a recommendation of the Robbins Report on Higher Education in 1963. This was the introduction of a first degree course in education, the Bachelor in Education (B.Ed.), the courses for which were to be taught by the colleges and the examinations for which were to be run in conjunction with the universities. The intention was that college lecturers were to be recognized as teaching to university standard. Most universities acted upon this suggestion of the Robbins Report very quickly. Other changes were made

[1] *Higher Education*, 1963, p. 15; *Statistics of Education*, Part II, 1965, p. 119.
[2] *Education in 1960*, 1961, p. 72.

following this report in the endeavour to create a situation where the colleges could gain a position nearer parity with the universities. The name 'training college' was associated with the elementary code and low status. The three-year course enabled more stress to be put on education and relatively less on training. The colleges therefore reacted quickly to the recommendation that their name should be changed to 'Colleges of Education'. In addition, their new relationship to the universities demanded a structure of college government more akin to that of the universities. Two innovations followed. The first related to internal government; many colleges set up academic boards to enable the staff to have a greater share with their Principals in running their colleges. Secondly, arrangements were made, more particularly in the case of L.E.A. colleges which had traditionally been closely controlled by their local government authority, to enable the colleges to become more self-governing in nature. Of especial importance here was the absolute freedom to recruit to their staffs whom they thought fit; this right had not always been allowed colleges in the past.

The new College of Education is becoming a very different place from the old training college. Apart from the changes already mentioned the colleges have grown greatly in size. Between 1958/9 and 1962/3 the number of colleges with less than 250 students fell from 98 to 46.[1] Several colleges now have over 1,000 students. Two consequences follow. There has been movement away from the former maternalistic method whereby one lecturer was responsible for much of a student's work, particularly in the field of education, throughout the two years, to a more specialized system whereby students receive the benefit of the teaching of experts in the disciplines such as psychology, sociology, history and philosophy that are especially relevant to the field of education. In addition this increased scope for a finer division of labour among the teaching staff has enabled the other parts of the course to become richer in content, as specialists in subjects formerly not taught can now find a place on the larger staffs.

The expansion of the universities in Britain has also been

[1] *Higher Education*, 1963, p. 110.

great. Whereas in 1938 1·7 per cent of the age group entered university, in 1954 3·4 per cent and in 1962 4·1 per cent entered. In absolute terms numbers at universities rose between 1954 and 1962 from 82,000 to 118,000.[1] Yet despite this absolute and relative growth the chances of working-class children reaching university apparently have not risen over the period since the 1944 Act. In view of the known quantity of young persons from lower social classes who are capable of reaching university it would seem that the educational system is not working well at this point in its function of selecting talent.

Another failure was the way the universities reacted slowly to the needs of the economy. The criteria by which this may be measured is the relative rates of growth in different university faculties. Thus, in the first post-war decade the numbers of degrees given in all faculties rose except for those in faculties of technology which by 1956 had therefore suffered a relative decline. It was only after the 1956 White Paper that during the second post-war decade the numbers of graduates in the applied sciences rose. The increase in both pure and applied science students has to some extent been held back by the shortage of sixth-formers qualified in the basic scientific subjects needed for these university courses. Indeed in the 1960s the numbers of those in sixth forms studying these subjects actually began to fall.

The expansion of the universities was accomplished partly by developing existing universities and partly by starting new ones. The university colleges that had been created in the inter-war years, as for example Leicester, had taught students for London external degrees. These colleges became universities. London, having colonized the provinces academically, turned its attention to assisting the growth of the universities of former colonial territories. New universities were founded in many parts of the country. These universities gained their royal charters immediately without any period of apprenticeship, and this gave them freedom to plan courses unhampered by the need to meet the requirements of a London external degree. This had a liberating effect and universities like Sussex and Essex made every attempt

[1] *Higher Education*, 1963, pp. 15 and 16.

to cross subject boundaries, studying, for instance, the whole culture of a foreign country rather than merely its language or its history. The attempts to break new ground proved very popular, since able students were attracted and staff of great talent were drawn away from such traditional centres of excellence as Oxford and Cambridge.

One way of summarizing the great overall growth in education during the period following the 1944 Act is by measuring the increasing proportion of the national income spent on education by public authorities. The second post-war decade saw the most rapid rise. In 1954/5 3·2 per cent of the gross national product went to education; by 1964/5 the figure had risen to 5·1 per cent.[1] Though some primary schools were still old, many were new, and in the vast majority, even of the older ones, the spirit of 'primary' education was very different from the old 'elementary' tradition. Children all went forward to a free secondary education and, though regional inequalities existed in the proportions of places available in selective schools, gross inequalities in social class chances of reaching grammar school had been eliminated. Furthermore, the question had now been asked whether this achievement was in itself the way to guarantee equality. One reason for this new doubt was the realization that the new Secondary Modern School could not be given parity of esteem. This had to be earned and the Modern School was too closely linked to groups in society that carried low status to earn esteem with ease. One answer to these problems seemed to be to reorganize secondary education by switching to some form of comprehensive system.

It was lack of status again that hindered the growth of technical education during the first post-war decade, though the needs of the economy forced a change after 1956. The new drive for applied scientists also affected the universities, where great growth in the other faculties had left the technological faculties unaffected. The increase in scientists from the universities was somewhat checked by a shortage of adequately qualified school leavers, and this in its turn depended on an adequate supply of teachers. One of the great growth points since 1944 has been in

[1] *Statistics of Education*, Part I, 1965, p. 73.

the training of teachers, but this has been in the supply of primary and secondary teachers other than mathematicians and scientists who remain relatively scarce. In this brief summary of the results of the 1944 Act certain strains have been mentioned – consideration must now be given to them.

2 Strains

For many reasons since 1945 economic considerations have been crucial to Britain. The policy of full employment has led to a tendency towards inflation, and this in its turn has brought recurrent difficulties with the balance of payments. Britain has had to use exports to pay for many more of her imports compared with before the war, since she had to service extensive debts incurred during the war. Strong foreign competition in our export markets has forced this country to take account of industrial efficiency as never before. An added influence in this direction in the 1960s was the preparation to join the European Common Market. Many comparisons have been made with the productivity of industry in the U.S.A., the U.S.S.R., and European countries, and particularly with these countries' use of trained manpower.

Full employment has brought a rapid rate of technological change. Industry is, therefore, now more firmly based on science and research. This change has increased the *per capita* wealth of the country and enabled the population to take some of their greater wealth as leisure. So education for leisure has come to be considered as important, especially when so many earn their greater leisure by performing work of little intrinsic interest. Education here can be seen as combating a feeling of alienation, but it is equally true to see education as an investment, since increased wealth will not be available unless the educational system produces sufficient highly trained manpower to meet the needs of the labour force.

The process by which industry comes to demand a labour force with a higher content of skill and education is at work throughout the occupational structure. Managers, technicians, foremen, apprentices and many operatives must have knowledge and skills that can only be taught by some formal means.

The educational needs of the economy are now very complex, including not just knowledge of the pure and applied sciences, but also skills in the newer social sciences and in such applied fields as secretarial work. Rapid technical change means that knowledge and skills become obsolete and retraining has grown essential, whether this is done by industry itself or in coopera- tion with the technical colleges. Attempts have been made to foresee the future needs of manpower by the economy. In the war, planning of the use of scarce resources of manpower had been vital, so that after the war it was easy to set up an advisory committee to examine the problems of supply of scientific and engineering manpower. Though this committee was not very accurate in its forecasts (and the same was true of similar committees on the supply of teachers and doctors), its reports initiated public discussion of this problem, namely the way in which the educational system should adapt to the needs of a rapidly changing society.

The additional labour required by the economy has come mainly from three sources and in each case there have been implications for education. Firstly, there have been immigrants, often from countries in the Commonwealth. Many of these new- comers have brought children whose prior education has been of a much lower standard than English children of a similar age and also, in many cases who only spoke their native tongue, thus creating problems in areas where immigrants have clustered. The second source has been the increased proportion of women in the labour force, as a result of which there has been a growing demand for nursery school provision and for the care of very young children that was normally associated with the family. Increased provision of school lunches, even in holiday times, has been necessary and arrangements have been made by some L.E.A.s to care for children in the day-time during school holidays.

These two sources of labour lead to a consideration of changes in the family. The average age of marriage has fallen and women have their children earlier. Since more stay longer at school, expectations of their future role have changed. There has come to be a great conflict between the roles to which most women are

123

ascribed, namely those of wife and mother, and the role which she herself achieves, namely that of worker. This conflict is present for almost all married women, but is perhaps more of a problem for middle-class women, whose education has usually been longer and who have a greater expectation of some form of professional career.

The third source of additional labour resulted from the post-war rise in the birth-rate. Since there was also a need for many women in the labour force, post-war parents often expected much more of the school. Some former functions of the family passed in some measure to the school. Much that the family taught became part of the school curriculum; for example, girls now often learnt to cook and sew at school rather than at home. In the nineteenth century the family had taught children such skills and also given many the motivation to achieve as adults. By the mid-twentieth century the family was unable to teach many of the complicated skills required by the economy, but the school not only was expected to teach these but also to inculcate much of the motivation that the child had formerly learnt at home. The moral responsibilities of the schools were further increased by the rise in crime among youth. In the decade after the war drunkenness among those aged seventeen to twenty rose fivefold, crimes of violence trebled and sexual offences doubled.

Children matured earlier physically and sexually. Many adolescents still at school no longer considered themselves as older children, but as young adults. Neither their families nor their schools were certain which role such young persons were playing. This doubt often led to disciplinary problems. Often teachers and others blamed the influence of the mass media, particularly the almost total coverage of television. Greater wealth also enabled young people to buy more books and comics, the effect of which on moral standards was uncertain. Many of the problems implicit in the almost simultaneous arrival of greater wealth and mass literacy have led to strains to which the family and the educational system have not as yet adapted.

In this social climate religion as an institution has come to have less importance than in the nineteenth century. Between

10 and 15 per cent of children are now estimated to attend at Sunday School. Yet the denominations still rate high their involvement in the dual system as it developed after the 1944 Act. So advantageous was this Act to the church schools that there was little pressure to disturb the truce of 1944, despite the difficulties encountered in financing more school places of the higher standard now required by Ministry regulations. In 1959 an Act was passed to ease the financial position of the denominations and further measures to this end were taken in 1966. However, there was a growing demand that religious instruction should cease to be given in the schools. This plea came mainly from the humanists, but despite the general lack of interest in, and of attendance at, the churches several surveys have shown that a majority of parents support religious instruction in the schools as a means of moral instruction.

In 1902, and even to some extent as late as 1944, education had entered the field of politics largely in terms of religious interests. But after 1945 education was increasingly considered politically in egalitarian terms, and hence the Labour Party championed an attack on privilege whilst the Conservatives, somewhat on the defensive, tried to make the existing tripartite system work more fairly. So great was the task of reconstruction undertaken by the Labour government between 1945 and 1950 that amidst all their other reforms merely to start the educational system developing along the lines of the definitions implicit in the 1944 Act was a large enough task. Between 1951 and 1964 the Conservatives were in power, and in opposition Labour began to realize that the 1944 Act was not achieving all that had been hoped. By 1964, though the number of grammar school places had risen greatly, it was clear that the proportion of working-class children in them was still much what it had been prior to 1944. One direct consequence was that the proportion of middle-class children at the universities was as large as ever; in fact, it had probably increased. Therefore, movement up the social class system, which was now largely dependent upon the formal educational qualifications gained at grammar school and needed by the economy, was little greater than it had been in the inter-war years.

At a time when many working-class parents had come to see the importance for their children of staying on at school beyond the legal minimum age for leaving, the system built to interpret the demand for 'Secondary education for all' was seen to be failing to meet their needs. Furthermore, it became apparent that, however fair the method of selection was for grammar or technical school, there was a large number of potentially able children whose capabilities were not developed by the tripartite system. Many of these children came from homes in socially disadvantageous areas. For these reasons the arguments for comprehensive schools became stronger.

In 1945 the Ministry published *A Guide to the Educational System of England and Wales* in which they wrote of 'three main alternative types of secondary education'. In the succeeding years the development plans of the L.E.A.s that were called for under the 1944 Act started to come into the Ministry. They were of various forms, but many of those from urban areas were cast in comprehensive form. This was particularly true where the areas had councils dominated by Labour. In 1947 the Ministry published another pamphlet, *The New Secondary Education*, in which they spoke of there being 'no set guides for organization', and in which they, for the first time, officially defined a comprehensive school. However, it was only in the 1950s that the demand for this new form of secondary school became really powerful and, though the Conservatives did not prohibit new schools being built as comprehensive schools, they did little to encourage such developments.

By the 1960s the definition of education that each social class gave had changed a great deal when compared with those that were implicit in the Act of 1944 upon which the educational system still rested. Many working-class people still did not want higher or even secondary education for their children, often for the very human reason that they realized what the effect of this would be, namely the moving of their children into a totally new world into which their parents could not follow. However, sufficient people did want a system that would be less élitist in nature than the tripartite system for their new definition to carry great political weight. Thus, the working-class definition of education became a common secondary education for all with higher education to follow for as many as possible. Those who went on to higher education were to receive liberal grants so that the minimum burden was put on poor parents. The policy of a common secondary school also implied the end of the fee-paying public school and, indeed, private schools came under increasing criticism during the later part of this period.

The middle class was now willing to bow to the political pressures for a fairer educational system and some even came to support the idea of a common school. Yet in the main they wished to retain the tripartite system and their own private educational system of preparatory and public schools which more often could lead to the older universities and to more promising jobs in industry than was the case with the grammar schools. Support for the grammar school was particularly strong in suburban areas, where the middle class are strongest. Yet in many such areas after 1961 Associations for the Advancement of State Education were founded as pressure groups with the aim of improving the local schools along the lines desired by their members, who seemed to be drawn mainly from middle-class professional groups. In some areas these groups pressed early for reorganization of secondary schools and were in general in favour of comprehensive schools.

As these new social class definitions of education became clearer during the 1950s, conflict was inevitable between a Ministry under Conservative control and the many L.E.A.s under Labour control. Only once did the final sanction, namely withdrawal of the Treasury grant, have to be threatened. This was in the case of Manchester in 1955, when the L.E.A. wished to incur expenditure in establishing two comprehensive schools in a way not permitted by the regulations. Since to pursue their policy would have meant a loss of half the finance needed for their school provision Manchester yielded. In 1965, after Labour had returned to power, the new government issued Circular 10/65, calling for plans for secondary reorganization on the basis of comprehensive schools. A few L.E.A.s showed marked reluctance to follow the policy of the central government and have declined to abandon the tripartite system.

By the 1960s education was a major issue at local and national level. Expenditure was high and looked as if it would rise. In this situation the issue of the efficient use of resources became important. There was a demand for the use of the techniques of cost analysis, not only in industry, but in the social services. Questions were raised such as the following: Why should the expensive buildings and capital equipment that was sunk by the nation in the universities and Colleges of Education remain idle through almost a quarter of each year? Why did failure rates vary so greatly in different educational institutions? What was the most efficient size for a primary school? And what was the cheapest way to build schools and other educational buildings? This was a totally new way to view education, and it was not surprising that during the 1950s the economics of education had differentiated out as a separate branch of economics.

This particular development was one example of a more general movement to consider education at least as much in its social, as in its individual, function. In response to these social pressures many within the educational system started to initiate changes in curricula and in methods. Two of the three R's received much attention. The Ministry's surveys found that reading standards were improving over the two post-war decades and soon the deterioration due to wartime disruptions were made good. Yet new ways of teaching children to read were still tried in the attempt to give every child from whatever social circumstances all opportunities to develop his capabilities. It was, however, in mathematics that the most experimenting took place. The underlying pressure here was the drive towards more complete 'numeracy' – a word coined by the Central Advisory's Crowther Report (1959) to parallel 'literacy'. The teaching of mathematics at primary level was rethought in the light of the findings of the Swiss psychologist, Piaget, with the aim of bringing children to a real understanding of mathematical principles rather than learning to operate rules by rote. New syllabuses were established at secondary level to take account of these changes. Two other pressures here were the shortage of mathematicians for industry and the influence of the electronic computer, which demanded understanding of a somewhat different mathematics from that taught formerly.

As psychologists discovered more of the way in which learning takes place new methods of encouraging children to learn in a much more active way were introduced into schools. Two examples may be cited. Firstly, teaching machines began to be used in some schools though on the whole they were more common in industrial training establishments. Secondly, in both modern language and science teaching great stress came to be put on learning by doing. The Nuffield Foundation financed the research for and development of new curricula in the various school subjects. Special science kits were devised so that children could experiment and find out for themselves. The pressure for science and mathematics in the schools affected both boys and girls, since under contemporary economic conditions girls as well as boys often needed this mental equipment to achieve success at work.

Teachers were both helped and hindered by the great growth of the mass media. Radio and television were used extensively as teaching aids. Sometimes, as in the case of science and mathematics, these media came to substitute for teachers with skills in short supply; lessons could be given to the children by experts whilst they were supervised by their own less expert teachers. But the media became powerful competitors to the teacher. Many advertisements could teach much more efficiently than teachers; methods had to be improved. In addition, most teachers did not approve of what the media, particularly the television, taught. They, therefore, came to see as part of their task the attempt to teach children to discriminate among the mass media messages that now formed their environment, thereby in some measure reasserting their individuality against the pressure towards cultural uniformity.

Prior to the war comparatively little research had been done in the field of education. The major effort had been in the field of psychological testing. The importance of the eleven plus examination had ensured that there was a continuance of this work after 1945. But greater stress was now put on educational research as a whole. The National Foundation for Educational

Research was established soon after the war, and in 1961 a Ministry of Education working party recommended a more active policy by the government in this field. The demand for greater egalitarianism both led to and was reinforced by sociological research into education, more especially by that on the chances of the various social classes of reaching grammar school and on the social determinants of educability.

Attitudes towards education changed after the war and became more favourable, mainly because of its clear connection with occupational success. To some extent the effect of this was that the status of teachers rose. The shortage of trained teachers put the N.U.T. in a strong position and the pay of teachers improved considerably in relation to similar occupations, though not to the extent many hoped for. In the first Burnham award after the war all teachers had been placed on the same scale as part of the attempt to give parity of esteem to all branches of the system. But the shortage of graduates, particularly with good honours degrees and with qualifications in mathematics or science, soon forced differentials to be reinstated to tempt men and women away from industry into the schools.

The shortage of teachers led to suggestions that the role of the teacher should be reassessed. In the nineteenth-century elementary school the teacher had dealt with the class as a whole all the time; in the twentieth-century secondary schools the teacher far more often taught specific subjects and even in the primary schools this had begun to happen in some measure. This development seemed to many to lead logically to a differentiation of the role of the teacher. The highly trained teacher would concentrate on his specialist task whilst a less qualified aide or auxiliary would assist him by performing tasks for which long training was not required. By the 1960s such aides were being employed in infant schools, though there was great opposition to this, as teachers feared that the profession would be diluted by unskilled labour.

In some respects the role of the teacher has undergone redefinition. A teacher may now be a part-time worker. One measure to cope with the shortage, especially at primary level, has been to employ as part-time teachers married former teachers whose children are now old enough to be left. This is a far cry from the fate of the married teacher in the inter-war years when marriage meant an end to teaching. Another change has been that teachers need no longer start their training at eighteen; mature men and women are encouraged to become teachers after working in other jobs. In addition, the need to ensure that children choose wisely among the occupations open to them on leaving school at a time when this choice is often more complex because of economic change has meant that many secondary schools have appointed specialist career masters and mistresses. The role of teacher is now less narrow as compared with before 1939.

In answer to the needs of the economy and the political demands for fairness a greater proportion of the nation's resources has been directed into education since 1945. Fuller employment of national capital has made greater wealth available for this purpose, but has put an additional strain on each level of the educational system. Coordination has become very difficult as the system has grown in complexity. New problems have arisen, such as, for instance, how to match the output of graduates from higher education to the needs of the economy or how to establish a linked system of schools that is as fair as possible for all social classes and in addition meets local needs. One key shortage of manpower has been the supply of teachers. Therefore, even to maintain the present pattern, were that desirable, would have been a problem. However, an increasing rate of social, as well as economic, change has affected such disparate fields as the role of women and the position of the mass media. Hence pressures have been put on the educational system to which it has been slow to adapt. These strains have been noted by many commentators and there has been a number of reconsiderations of the 1944 definition of education.

3 Redefinition

Since the state began to take a major part in the provision of education in England in 1870, a major goal has been to allow for as much local initiative as possible. However, since contemporary society is highly specialized and organized largely on a national level, the question arises how much local control over education can continue. Just over half of current expenditure by L.E.A.s is financed by the Treasury and most expenditure is governed by regulations made in London. The size of capital expenditure is such that control at national level is essential. For example, in the *School Building Survey (1962)*, published in 1965, it was estimated that the cost of bringing all buildings up to standard and of new buildings for raising the leaving age to sixteen would be £1,368 millions. Some of the smaller L.E.A.s that survived the 1944 Act did amalgamate with bigger areas in the early fifties and the reorganization of local government in the 1960s in the London area has had a similar effect. Indeed, the redefinition of the administrative responsibilities of L.E.A.s is very much dependent upon the major reconsideration of local government that has been undertaken in the 1960s.

Education has become a major sector of the economy. Around a million people are employed in this branch of the labour force, of whom over 300,000 are teachers. Much capital is invested yearly in the provision of education, and the main reason for this is that government expenditure on education is now defined as an investment in the nation's potentiality for faster economic growth. It was because of the close link between the economy and education that in 1959 the Crowther Report coined the word 'numeracy' to match the literacy that had been seen as vital to nineteenth-century economic growth. This report examined 'the education of boys and girls between the ages of 15 and 18' and gave much attention to science, mathematics and to technical education. This last sector was described as 'neglected educational territory'[1] and had not been considered in any detail by a government committee since the Samuelson Report of 1884. For the Crowther Committee the economic function of education was central. The Newsom Report of 1963, which considered 'the education of pupils aged 13 to 16 of average and less than average ability', also put great stress on the economic relevance of education. Secondary education for the less able child was defined as being 'practical, realistic, vocational'.[2] One administrative change is symbolic of this

---

[1] 15–18, Vol. I, 1959, p. 313.
[2] *Half Our Future*, 1963, p. 114.

trend. In 1959 a Ministry of Science was created, but in 1964 this was merged with the Ministry of Education to form the Department of Education and Science. The Department has taken a greater interest in the curricula of the schools and, despite the protests of teachers that this was an infringement of their freedom, in 1962 established the Curriculum Study Group which became in 1964 the Schools Council for Curriculum and Examinations. This body has financed research on the curriculum and on teaching methods, issued reports and is an example in the academic, as opposed to the financial, field of the centralizing tendencies in English education.

The increasing emphasis on the links between education and the economy has blurred the boundaries between these two social institutions. Many large industrial enterprises now run apprenticeship and other training schemes often with a high content of a purely educational nature. The passing of the Industrial Training Act in 1964 gave the Ministry of Labour powers to make levies on industries to encourage and finance training, to set standards, to organize examinations and to ensure the supply of the necessary teachers. Much of this work will necessitate the use of educational facilities and a definition of the limits of the responsibilities of the two institutions and of the method of coordination is needed.

The greater complexity of educational effort has increased the difficulties of coordination. An example has been given in the growth of the Youth Employment Service. In addition, the Youth Service, established in 1939, has been given more importance because of the increase in problems associated with adolescence. In 1960 the Albemarle Committee redefined the Youth Service as a part of educational provision.[1] As a consequence the Youth Development Council was created and more money given to this service. But implicit in this arrangement was a social definition of the adolescent as both a problem and a non-adult. Neither of these latent views on adolescence greatly helped the manifest difficulties involved in the transition from childhood to adulthood under contemporary conditions where moral values are uncertain and changing. Much thought

[1] *The Youth Service in England and Wales, 1960,* espec. Ch. IV.

133

has been given to this side of education. It was in this context that the Newsom Committee defined religious instruction as a central part of secondary education. 'Society must not look to the schools to solve its moral problems, but it expects and gets from them an important contribution towards this solution.'[1] Since contemporary educational provision has its roots in the dual system established in 1870, organized religion still has a vested interest in the ongoing process of redefining education in England.

The economy has had a conspicuous place in the redefinitions of education since 1945. Social class, has, however, been given prominence, particularly since the Central Advisory Council's report on *Early Leaving* in 1954. This showed the close connection between social class and leaving selective secondary schools at the minimum legal age before the first external examination. Yet in the discussions of educational policy social class seems now to have lost some of the ideological overtones that it formerly carried. In the *Early Leaving*, Crowther and Robbins Reports, though this is not true of the Newsom and Plowden[2] Reports, social class was mainly used in the analysis of the loss of talent, a problem given importance in an economic, as much as an egalitarian, context. Furthermore, much of the present case for the reorganization of secondary education, an issue completely avoided by Crowther and Newsom, has been based on similar arguments of an economic nature, though the ideological argument for egalitarianism has also been important. Both the Newsom and the Plowden Reports have drawn attention to the problem of education in slum areas. Children in schools in these areas cannot be given an equal chance of a full secondary education by reorganizing the secondary schools on some comprehensive plan unless the damage done in their early years because of deprivation in the family is offset. This may be achieved by nursery schools, particularly as the proportion of working mothers is high in such areas. In 1967 the Plowden Committee redefined fairness in such a way that these disadvantaged areas should be given a greater share of educational

[1] *Half Our Future*, 1963, p. 53.
[2] *Children and their Primary Schools*, 1967.

facilities than other areas in order that children might have a chance to overcome their environment.

The redefinitions of secondary education that have been made by these reports have been in terms of curriculum, teaching methods, and internal organization of the schools, not in terms of the reorganization of the system away from the tripartitism assumed by the 1944 Act. Economic and administrative, rather than egalitarian, considerations have been given most weight. No official definition of the problems connected with fairness took place until the Labour Party came to power, when in 1965 the Department of Education and Science issued Circular 10/65 indicating that reorganization should take place along a number of possible lines, all of which could be subsumed under the term 'comprehensive'. This raised the problem of the public schools, since, even if the state system was totally reorganized on comprehensive lines, it would still be possible for parents to opt out as long as a parallel private system of schools continued to exist. The government, therefore, appointed a royal commission under Sir John Newsom to attempt to define the relationship of the public schools to the state educational system.

Nowhere has the prominence of the economy been seen more clearly in recent redefinitions of education than in the Robbins Report on Higher Education. Here the first 'objective essential to any properly balanced system' was seen to be 'instruction in skills suitable to play a part in the general division of labour'. It was fourth and last and only as part of 'the transmission of a common culture' that 'the ideal of equality of opportunity' was mentioned.[1] The rising proportion of the labour force in the managerial and administrative sector and the explosion of knowledge due to the increase in research forced this emphasis. The definition of higher education made by the Robbins Committee was a new one in that it viewed the universities and the technical and training colleges as a unity and wished both types of colleges to be modelled on the universities.

Measures have been taken to apply this definition to the system by converting the Colleges of Advanced Technology into universities and in renaming the training colleges as Colleges of

[1] *Higher Education,* 1963, pp. 6–7.

135

Education with some work of degree standard and more independent means of self-government. Yet there were other problems. The Robbins committee did not consider the whole sector of professional education, often of degree level, which is pursued outside the universities, and usually in technical colleges just below the level of the former Colleges of Advanced Technology. The education of engineers of many types is an example. The Labour government has taken steps to define such education into the university level by establishing a competitor to the university system, the Council for National Academic Awards. This body approves curricula submitted from technical colleges and awards degrees, so that by the mid-1960s a so-called 'Binary system' was emerging. The higher-status and higher-cost universities function alongside the less prestigious and cheaper technical colleges, both supplying higher education. Relevant to this development is the reassessment of the position of the Universities Grants Committee. In 1962/3 public spending on university education was £129 millions and was increasing yearly. A strong body of political opinion felt that expenditure at such a rate should be under more direct control than was possible through the Grants Committee. Fundamentally, the demand was that the universities should be brought into the educational system in the fullest sense as, in fact, is the other arm of the binary system of higher education.

4 Conclusion

When the school-leaving age is raised to sixteen in 1972, all the provisions of the 1944 Act will have been carried out with one exception. Once again the day release clauses have been left unaccomplished, though the Industrial Training Act may have a rather similar effect to the imposition of compulsory day release. Yet many strains, unforeseen in 1944, have been at work and there are strains that have brought the system close to the threshold of redefinition. The present analysis indicates that the relative importance of the various social institutions impinging upon English education today is such that the next definition of the educational situation will be much more influenced by economic and administrative interests and much less by organized religion than has been the case at any of the three major truce situations since 1870. Indeed, so important is the economy that the universities may find themselves defined merely as one group of organizations within the general tertiary sector, rather than as special organizations outside the general definition of educational provision. The other mainspring of the process whereby education has been constantly redefined over the last century, namely the demand for egalitarianism, is now no longer relatively so prominent as was the case at the time of past definitions. Its final major achievement may be legislation that defines the public school as a part of the educational system. Until the public schools and the universities, to which so much both of a useful and of a harmful nature is owed by the English educational system, are both comprehended in some way within the state system, there will not exist the unitary educational system towards which England seems to have been moving over the last century.

CHAPTER SIX

CONCLUSIONS

The development of the definitions of education in England over the last hundred years has been marked by a sense of continuity; change has come about in an evolutionary way. Different social systems or institutions can tolerate different levels of internal conflict. In education, goals particularly at societal level are vague, as for instance the demand for secondary education for all. It is, therefore, easy for the schools to justify to the public as legitimate their interpretation of any definition. This intrinsic vagueness is one source of change within an educational system, but in England there has been an additional source. The strong support of the ideology of *laissez-faire* has made possible a wide range of tolerance in the three major definitions of education made in 1870, 1902 and 1944, thereby permitting an ongoing process of minor redefinition. Since 1899 this process has been made official by the creation of the Consultative Council (later the Central Advisory Committees). The reports of these bodies have given quasi-official standing to the many minor redefinitions of sectors of the educational system that otherwise might not have gained easy recognition. This piecemeal method of redefinition has given continuity between major definitions of education and enabled educational revolutions to take place in an evolutionary setting.

Once definitions have become law or have been assumed as the basis for law, as was the case with tripartitism at the time of the

1944 Act, resources flow into education. As the status of education has risen through the last hundred years the proportion of the nation's income devoted to education has increased. Several consequences have followed. The role of the teacher has changed considerably. The elementary teacher had a diffuse responsibility for his pupil, whereas today certainly the secondary, and to some extent even the primary, teacher has a specialist and particular role oriented towards an instrumental view of education as the major means of achieving success under contemporary economic conditions. Many of the former responsibilities of the teacher have been transferred to such specialists as the Youth Employment Officer, school doctor or a representative of some welfare agency.

The educational system has grown increasingly differentiated and this raises questions of where its boundaries lie. Furthermore, within the system itself the boundaries of sub-systems become vague. Examples of this latter problem can be found in the inroads the Department of Science and Art made into secondary education at the end of the nineteenth century. The blurring of the boundaries of the larger social institutions is illustrated by the problems implicit in implementing the Industrial Training Act of 1964; in this case both the economy and education are tackling educational tasks. The coordination of various parts of the educational system has been eased by the creation of special representative committees such as the Schools Council and various Research Committees running, for instance, the Nuffield science and mathematics projects. These new organizational forms are one answer to the slow rate of adaptation to social change that the educational system has shown over the last hundred years, particularly in matching the school curriculum to the needs of other social institutions such as the economy or the family. A body like the Advisory Committee on Scientific Policy also serves an important social function in attempting to correct unbalanced growth such as has been common in the relationship between secondary and both higher and technical education.

The problem of where the threshold of redefinition lies is difficult of solution. In the English situation the accumulation of many small discrete changes has occurred and the final impulse to major redefinition has depended on the contemporary situation, though in 1902, 1918 and 1944 war also played a part. The particular power groups and particular institutions between which there are major strains are vital here. From the 1870s to the 1960s there has been a switch from social class and religion to the economy and administration as having major importance. Power groups use their influence within the climate of opinion ruling at any time and the truce situations arrived at in defining education have been governed by the attitudes to education held by the various social classes throughout the period. The general attitude towards change has also been important in allowing a new definition to take place or not. Lastly, as the claims of the economy have grown in relative importance, attitudes towards the application of science and education to industry have become crucial.

The more clearly the vital perspectives at the moment of definition are perceived, the more will the resulting system be adapted to the actual needs of the overall social system. Thus, in 1944 the latent egalitarian vision of the situation was missed and the implicit definition of secondary education as tripartite soon led to strains. The capacity to see these perspectives is complicated by the differing rates of change of the various social institutions that interlock with education. For example, inasmuch as a true measurement is possible, it seems that economic change was slower than political change in the inter-war years, whilst the reverse was the case after 1945 when change in the economy became the focus for education as for much else in England. Throughout these two periods the institution of religion changed at a very slow rate.

The direction of change in education is largely determined by what has happened in other major social institutions, though education in its turn can govern change elsewhere. It is only by studying the present relationships between education and these other institutions and by looking at the historical development of these relationships that any attempt can be made to foresee the possible future pathways of the educational system. Such prediction is made more difficult since the generation in power

views the contemporary position through the perspective learnt
in its youth. It was in this way that in the 1940s and 1950s
secondary education for all was defined in the tripartite terms of
the 1920s and 1930s. It is this type of problem of interpretation
that each generation faces as it looks to the future and tries to
define the most socially apt education for the next generation.
At the centre of this process of definition stands the teacher
whose role is governed by past and present definitions of education and whose work is often made more difficult by the strains
between education and other social institutions that will ultimately lead to redefinition. He must understand the process that
governs his task if he wishes to succeed in it.

FURTHER READING

I Primary sources

Readers are directed to the primary sources indicated in this book. The reports of the Royal Commissions and Advisory Committees/Councils are invaluable material for any fuller study of the development of English education over this period. Particular mention must be made of:

G. Baron, *A Bibliographical Guide to the English Educational System*, 3rd edition, 1965.

J. S. Maclure, *Educational Documents, England and Wales, 1816–1963*, 1965.

II Secondary sources

The following historical and sociological works are some of the many in the field and nearly all contain further references that may be followed up:

(*a*) *Historical*

M. Argles, *South Kensington to Robbins*, 1965.

W. H. G. Armytage, *Four Hundred Years of English Education*, 1964.

W. H. G. Armytage, *Civic Universities: Aspects of a British Tradition*, 1955.

E. Ashby, *Technology and the Academics*, 1958.

G. Baron, *Society, Schools and Progress in England*, 1965.

M. Cruickshank, *Church and State in English Education*, 1963.

P. H. J. H. Gosden, *The Development of Educational Administration in England and Wales*, 1966.

A. J. Peters, 'The Changing Idea of Technical Education', *British Journal of Educational Studies*, May 1963.

M. Sturt, *The Education of the People*, 1967.

(b) Sociological

O. Banks, *Parity and Prestige in English Secondary Education*, 1955.

R. G. Corwin, *A Sociology of Education* (especially Parts I, II and III), 1965.

S. F. Cotgrove, *Technical Education and Social Changes*, 1958.

D. V. Glass, 'Education and Social Change in Modern England', in A. H. Halsey, J. E. Floud and C. A. Anderson (eds.), *Education, Economy and Society*, 1961.

A. H. Halsey, 'British Universities and Intellectual Life', in A. H. Halsey, J. E. Floud and C. A. Anderson, op. cit.

A. H. Halsey, 'The Changing Functions of Universities', in A. H. Halsey, J. E. Floud and C. A. Anderson, op. cit.

G. Duncan Mitchell, 'Education, Ideology and Social Change', in G. K. Zollschen and W. Hirsch (eds.), *Explorations in Social Change*, 1964.

P. W. Musgrave, 'Constant Factors in the Demand for Technical Education, 1860–1960', *British Journal of Educational Studies*, May 1966.

P. W. Musgrave, *Technical Change, the Labour Force and Education*, 1967.

F. Musgrove, *The Migratory Elite*, 1963.

F. Musgrove, *Youth and the Social Order*, 1964.

A. Tropp, *The School Teachers*, 1957.

R. H. Turner, 'Modes of Social Ascent through Education: Sponsored and Contest Mobility', in A. H. Halsey, J. E. Floud and C. A. Anderson, op. cit.

R. Williams, *The Long Revolution*, 1961.

III More Detailed References

The following books and articles refer to more particular topics in individual chapters:

Further Reading

Chapter II

W. S. Fowler, 'The Origin of the General Certificate', *British Journal of Educational Studies*, May 1959.

F. Musgrove, 'Middle class education and employment in the nineteenth century', *Economic History Review*, August 1959.

F. Musgrove, 'Decline of the Educative Family', *Universities Quarterly*, September 1960.

D. Newsome, *Godliness and Good Learning*, 1961.

R. Rich, *The Training of Teachers in the Nineteenth Century*, 1933

J. Roach, 'Middle Class Education and Examinations', *British Journal of Educational Studies*, May, 1962.

H. Silver, *The Concept of Popular Education*, 1965.

B. Simon, *Studies in the History of Education, 1780–1870*, 1960.

R. K. Webb, *The British Working Class Reader, 1790–1848*, 1955.

Chapter III

M. Argles, 'The Royal Commission on Technical Instruction, 1881–4: its inception and composition', *Vocational Aspect*, Autumn 1959.

W. H. G. Armytage, 'J. D. F. Donnelly. Pioneer in vocational education', *Vocational Aspect*, May 1950.

G. Baron, 'Some Aspects of the "Headmaster Tradition" ', *Leeds Researches and Studies*, June 1956.

E. J. R. Eaglesham, *From School Board to Local Authority*, 1956.

P. W. Musgrave, 'The definition of technical education, 1860–1910, *Vocational Aspect*, May 1964.

A. Rodgers, 'Churches and Children', *British Journal of Educational Studies*, November 1959.

B. Simon, *Education and the Labour Movement, 1870–1920*, 1965.

Chapter IV

G. Bernbaum, *Social Change and the Schools, 1918–1944*, 1967.

C. Cannon, 'The Influence of Religion on Educational Policy, 1902–1914', *British Journal of Educational Studies*, May 1964.

B. Doherty, 'Compulsory Day Continuation Education: An Examination of the 1918 Experiment', *Vocational Aspect*, Spring 1966.

144

E. J. R. Eaglesham, 'Implementing the Education Act of 1962', *British Journal of Educational Studies*, May 1962.

E. J. R. Eaglesham, 'The Centenary of Sir Robert Morant', *British Journal of Educational Studies*, November 1963.

J. E. Floud, 'The Educational Experience of the Adult Population of England and Wales as at July, 1949', in D. V. Glass (ed.), *Social Mobility in Britain*, 1954.

F. E. Foden, 'The National Certificate', *Vocational Aspect*, May 1951.

A. V. Judges, 'The Educational Influence of the Webbs', *British Journal of Educational Studies*, November 1961.

A. Shakoor, *The Training of Teachers in England and Wales, 1900–1939*, unpublished Ph.D. thesis, University of Leicester, 1964.

J. W. Tibble, 'Psychological Theories and Teacher Training', in *Yearbook of Education, 1963*.

J. Vaizey, *The Costs of Education*, 1958.

D. E. Wheatley, 'City and Guilds Examinations', *Vocational Aspect*, Spring 1959.

Chapter V

H. C. Dent, *Growth in English Education, 1946–52*, 1954.

A. V. Judges, 'Tradition and the Comprehensive School', *British Journal of Educational Studies*, November 1953.

T. H. Marshall, 'Social Selection in the Welfare State', in A. H. Halsey, J. E. Floud and C. A. Anderson, op. cit.

G. I. Payne, *Britain's Scientific and Technological Manpower*, 1960.

R. Pedley, *The Comprehensive School*, 1963.

W. Taylor, *The Secondary Modern School*, 1963.

INDEX

147

Index

Index

truce situation, 2–4, 27, 42, 43, 58, 67, 72, 75, 140
tutors, 12, 16

U.S.A., 57, 89, 92, 122
universities, 16, 34, 41, 43, 49, 52, 53–55, 57, 58, 73, 75, 77, 85, 88–89, 91, 104, 105, 113, 117, 118, 119–21, 125, 128, 135, 136, 137
London, 17, 18, 34, 53, 55, 89, 117, 120
Oxford and Cambridge, 17, 18, 33, 34, 47, 53, 54, 57, 74, 75, 78, 85, 89, 113, 121, 127
Scottish, 65
Universities' Grants Committee, 75, 89, 104, 136

Vice-President of Committee of Privy Council, 25, 41, 45, 49
Voluntary Schools, 44, 45, 48, 63, 70

wars:
Boer, 64, 140
Napoleonic, 9, 12, 20
1914–1918, 77, 78, 81, 84, 87, 89, 91, 98, 102, 105, 140
1939–1945, 78, 82, 97, 101–2, 106, 108, 110, 140
Webb, Sidney, 44, 60, 62
Beatrice, 60, 62
'Whisky Money', 68–69
Winchester College, 15, 16, 38

Youth Employment Service, 80, 116, 133, 139
Youth Service, 116, 133

152